Eastern Shore of Maryland
The Guidebook

Katie Moose

Photographs by George and Katie Moose

Conduit Press
Annapolis, Maryland

Cover Photo: George Howard Moose, Jr.

Published by the Conduit Press, 111 Conduit Street, Annapolis, Maryland 21401.

Library of Congress Cataloging-in-Publication Data

Printed and Bound by United Book Press, Inc., Baltimore, Maryland, USA

ISBN: 0-9666610-2-8

Eastern Shore Table of Contents

Eastern Shore Illustrations

Chesapeake Exploration Center, Kent Island

Introduction

Maryland's Eastern Shore is connected to the state of Maryland by the Bay Bridge from the West and the state of Delaware to the East. To the south is Virginia. There are an abundance of creeks, peninsulas, islands, wildlife, oystering and crabbing, watermen, and tobacco and other types of plantations. People are proud of their love of the water and where a slower lifestyle exists.

Days can be spent wandering among these places, taking in some antique shops and sightseeing along the way. Ferries and bridges, many of them drawbridges, cross the numerous rivers and creeks. You truly do not know what will appear around the next corner. The "Traveling Brushes", a group of Eastern Shore ladies may be painting on an obscure creek, or cruising aboard a skipjack. Geese may fly over, heading north or south. But almost everywhere you look there are large farms producing wheat, corn, soybeans, tomatoes and other produce. Clumps of trees appear periodically. Gracious old farmhouses, some dating to the 1600s, are often not far from the road or down an allee of trees dating to the same period. Farther on may be a tumbling down farmhouse, still inhabited by members of the original family.

The Eastern Shore has some of the most elegant inns, B&Bs and restaurants in the United States. The region is home to some of the oldest churches, buildings, homes and plantations (some date back to the 17th century), and oldest shipyards.

This book explores the cities, towns and villages that make up the Eastern Shore. Each capsule contains the history, historic and not so historic sites, lodging and dining. The book starts by crossing the Bay Bridge, heading north to Chesapeake City, then south to Wye Mills and on down to Ocean City and finally ending up in Crisfield. There are a couple of very special places to stop along the way. The Old Grist Mill in Wye Mills is one of the oldest buildings in Maryland still operating as a grist mill. The Chesapeake Bay Maritime Museum in St. Michael's highlights the Bay's nautical and waterfowl history. But even more unique is the Ward Museum of Wildfowl Art in Salisbury. All three warrant a visit.

Have fun and please hope that this pristine countryside will not become one huge development. The metropolis of Washington, Baltimore, Philadelphia and Wilmington are fast encroaching on these tidewater shores. Captain John Smith would not recognize them today.

Chapter 1

Saturday Farmer's Market, St. Michael's

Informative Tips about the Eastern Shore

Traveling to the Eastern Shore

The easiest way to get around the Eastern Shore is by car. From Wilmington, and other northern points, or from the south take Rte. 301. From Washington or Baltimore Rte. 50 crosses the Bay Bridge to the Eastern Shore. From Norfolk take the Bay Bridge-Tunnel. On these routes and other main roads the speed limit is 55. In towns and villages the speed is 15-35. Please obey these rules.

One of the loveliest routes is to take Rte. 213 north or south. From the north you will see Chesapeake City, Georgetown, Chestertown, Centreville and on down to Wye Mills, plus other historic towns in between. From Route 50 you can go from Kent Island all the way to Ocean City.

The Eastern Shore is so vast that even a week will not cover all the wonderful towns, coves, creeks and historic places that make it so unique. One way to really see it is by boat, but even then enough time must be allowed to get from place to place. There is a chapter for those who chose to do so.

Welcome and Information Centers are located on 301 near Carville; Sailwinds Park in Cambridge; the Ocean City Information Center, off Rte. 50; and at the Chesapeake Exploration Center, Kent Island.

Calendar of Events

January

Ocean City Hot Rod and Custom Car Show
Nautical Wildlife Art Festival. Ocean City

February

Seaside Boat Show. Ocean City

March

St. Patrick's Day Parades

April

Chesapeake Bay Spring Boat Show. Bay Bridge Marina, Kent Island
International Car Show of the Eastern Shore. Ocean City
Ward World Championship Wildfowl Carving Competition. Ocean City
Annual Daffodil Show. Somerset County
Talbot County Charity Antiques Show & Sale. Easton
Classic Boat Show. Richardson Maritime Museum. Cambridge
Oxford Day. Oxford

May

Bay Bridge Walk
Salisbury Dogwood Festival

Maryland House and Garden Pilgrimage (may also be held in April)
Historic House & Garden Tour. St. Michael's
Chestertown Flower Mart
Chestertown Tea Party Festival. Historical re-enactments, parade, music, craft.
Vienna Heritage Celebration
Soft Shell Spring Fair. Crisfield
Kent Island Day
Memorial Day Parades
Greensboro Founder's Day Festival. 2nd Saturday
Strawberry Festival. Ridgely . Sunday before Memorial Day
Fairmount Academy Annual 1800s Festival. Fairmount

June

Bay Bridge Swim
Classic Boat Show. Chesapeake Bay Maritime Museum, St. Michael's
Tilghman Island Seafood Festival
Rock Hall Fish Tournament. Bulk Head, Rock Hall
Garden Tours, Chestertown
Eastern Shore Chamber Music Festival
Crumpton Garden Tour and Auction
Queen Anne's County Watermen's Festival. Grasonville
Bay Country Music Festival. Centreville
Berlin Village Fair
Cypress Festival. Pocomoke City
Talbot County Charity Antiques Show & Sale
Canal Day. Chesapeake City
Scorchy Tawes Pro-Am Fishing Tournament. Crisfield

July

Every town on the Eastern Shore sports special Fourth of July festivities. In addition many towns have evening band concerts. Please check local calendars.
Big Band Concert. St. Michael's
J. Millard Tawes Crab & Clam Bake. Crisfield
Kent County Fair
Pony Penning. Assateague Island
Cambridge Classic Powerboat Regatta
National Hard Crab Derby & Fair. Crisfield
Talbot County Fair
Smith Island Day. Ewell
Somerset County Fair. Civic Center. Princess Anne
Patriotic Xtravaganza. Federalsburg. Saturday before July 4th

August

Thunder on the Narrows. Powerboat races
Crab Derby. Crisfield
Betterton Day Celebration. 1st Saturday
Caroline County Fair
Worcester County Fair
Dorchester Chamber Seafood Feast-i-val. Cambridge
The Great Pocomoke Fair. Pocomoke City
Party on the Bay. Rock Hall
Threshermen's Festival. Federalsburg. 1st weekend
Caroline Summerfest. Denton

September

Skipjack Races. Off Deal Island
Candlelight Walking Tour. Chestertown
Pemberton Colonial Fair. Salisbury
National Hard Crab Derby and Fair. Crisfield
Chestertown Jazz Festival
Nause Waiwash, Annual Native American Festival. Cambridge
Eastern Shore Fall Festival Championship Jousting Tournament. Ridgely
African-American Heritage Festival. Berlin. 2nd Sunday

October

Tilghman Island Day
Olde Princess Anne Days. 2nd week in October. Tour of historic homes.
Chestertown Wildlife Show & Sale. Chestertown
Eastern Neck National Wildlife Refuge Week
Three Centuries of Kent Driving Tour
J. Millard Tawes Oyster and Bull Roast. Crisfield
Ward Foundation Exhibition. Salisbury
Carving Competition. Ocean City
Rock Hall Fallfest
Chesapeake Celtic Festival. Snow Hill
Native American Indian Heritage Festival and Pow-wow. Marion

November

Waterfowl Festival. Easton
Chestertown Festival of Trees
Festival of Trees. Easton
Festival of Trees. Salisbury

Holiday River Lights on the Choptank. Cambridge
OysterFest. Chesapeake Bay Maritime Museum. St. Michael's
Winterfest of lights. Ocean City

December

Colonial Christmas in Princess Anne. Candlelight tour
Christmas in Rock Hall
Holiday House Tours. Chestertown and Kent County
First Night Talbot. Easton
Christmas Candlelight Tour. Cambridge
Crumpton Candlelight House Tour
Vienna Candlelight Tour
Candlelight House Tour. Chesapeake City
Federalsburg Christmas Celebrations
Lighting of the Green. Denton
Ridgely Old-Fashioned Christmas. 1st Saturday
Martinak State Park. Santa's Magic Workshop
Christmas in Crisfield
Christmas in St. Michael's
Berlin's Victorian Christmas
Candlelight Home and Church Tour. Quantico
Victorian Christmas Celebration. Snow Hill
Christmas in Caroline. Denton

Important Numbers

Please remember that all numbers in area code 410 must have the 410 prefix to dial into that number.

Emergency	911
Maryland Poison Center	1-800-492-2414
U.S. Coast Guard	1-800-418-7314

Airports

The nearest major airport is BWI between Baltimore and Washington.
Easton Airport. 29137 Newman Road. 410-822-8560
Queen Anne's County Bay Bridge Airport. 202 Airport Road. Stevensville. 410-643-4364

Salisbury-Ocean City-Wicomico Regional Airport. 5485 Airport Terminal Road. Salisbury. 410-548-4827
Cambridge Airport-Dorchester. 5223Bucktown Road, Cambridge. 410-228-4571
Crisfield-Somerset County Airport. 4784 Jacksonville Road. Crisfield. 410-968-3062
Ocean City Airport. Rte. 611. 410-213-2471

Car Rentals

Avis. Easton Airport. 410-822-5040
Hertz. Goldsborough Road. Easton. 410-822-1676
Hertz . 800-654-3131
Sears. 1-800-527-0770
Enterprise Rent-A-Car. 1-800-325-8007
Avis. 800-831-2847
Alamo. 800-327-9633
Thrifty. 1-800-367-2277
Dollar. 1-800-800-4000

Taxis/Limousines

Scotty's Taxi. Easton. 410-822-1475
Eastern Shore Limousine Service. Easton. 800-453-2023
The Travel Associates. Easton. 410-822-4686

Motorcoach Transportation

Pritchett's Transportation Company, Inc. Cambridge. 410-228-6907
Tidewater Motorcoach, LLC. Cambridge. 410-228-5026
Kirby Tours. Denton. 410-479-2551

Bus Lines

Dillons Bus Company. 1-800-827-3490
Dorsey Bus Service. 410-778-0138
Greyhound/Trailways. 800-231-2222
Somerset Commuter. Westover. 410-651-1120

Walking Tours

Almost every town on the Eastern Shore has a good walking tour map and many conduct walking tours.

Visitor Centers and Chambers of Commerce

Talbot County Conference and Visitors Bureau. 11 N. Washington Street. Easton. 888-BAY-STAY
Dorchester County Tourism Department. 2 Rose Hill Place. Cambridge. 410-228-1000
Kent County Chamber of Commerce. Chestertown. 410-778-0416
Queen Anne County Office of Business and Tourism. 425 Piney Narrows Road. Chester. 410-604-2100
Wicomico County Convention and Visitors Bureau. 8480 Ocean Highway. Salisbury. 410-548-4914
Caroline County Office of Tourism. 218 Market Street. Denton. 410-479-0660
Somerset County Tourism. Box 243. Princess Anne. 410-651-2968
Worcester County Tourism. 105 Pearl Street. Snow Hill. 410-852-0335
Cecil County Tourism. Rm. 324, 129 E. Main Street. Elkton. 410-996-5303
Ocean City Convention and Visitors Bureau. 4001 Coastal Highway. Ocean City. 410-289-8181

Special Organizations

Almost every town has an historical society. These maintain some of the lovely old buildings and are usually housed in an historical building.
Eastern Shore Land Conservancy. Queenstown. 410-827-9756
Chester River Association. Chestertown. 410-827-9756

Newspapers

Baltimore Sun. 501 N. Calvert Street. Baltimore. 410-332-6000
Washington Post. 1150 15th Street, NW, Washington, DC. 202-334-6000
The Washington Times. 3600 New York Avenue, Washington, DC. 202-269-3419
The Easton Star-Democrat. One Airport Park. Easton. 410-822-1500
The Daily Banner. 1000 Goodwill Road. Cambridge. 410-228-3131
Kent County News. 217 High Street. Chestertown. 410-778-2011

The Dorchester Star. 300 Academy Street. Cambridge. 410-228-0222
Somerset Herald. Somerset Avenue and Prince William Street. Princess Anne. 410-651-1600
Maryland Coast Dispatch. Berlin. 410-641-4561
Somerset/Crisfield Express. 1021 Old Princess Anne Road. Princess Anne. 410-289-6834
The Daily Times. Times Square. Salisbury. 410-749-7171
The News & Advertiser. E. Market Street. Salisbury
Cecil Whig.

Magazines

Tidewater Times. Oxford Maryland. 410-226-0422. This delightful little magazine is published monthly and contains interesting tidbits on the Eastern Shore.
Chesapeake Bay Magazine. 1819 Bay Ridge Avenue. Annapolis. 410-263-2662
Chesapeake

Radio/TV Stations

WCEM-AM-1240 – Cambridge – Country, news
WCTR-AM-1530 – Chestertown – Talk shows, news, sports,
WKDI-AM-840 – Denton – Religious
WCEI-AM-1460 – Easton – Talk, easy listening
WCEI-FM-96.7 – Easton
WAAI-FM-100.9 – Hurlock – Country
WESM-FM-91.3 – University of Maryland Eastern Shore
WOLC-FM-102.5 – Princess Anne – Religious
WBOC-TV-16 – Salisbury
WCPB-TV-28 – Salisbury Public Broadcasting
WDIH-FM-90.3 – Contemporary
WICO-AM-1320 – Salisbury – Talk, news, sports
WJDY-AM-1470 – Contemporary
WMDT-TV-47 – Salisbury
WQHQ-FM-104.7 – Salisbury - Contemporary
WSBY-FM-98.9 – Salisbury – Oldies
WSCL-FM-89.5 – Salisbury – Classical
WTGM-AM-960 – Salisbury – Sports
WWFG-FM-99.9 - Country

Hospitals

Kent & Queen Anne's Hospital, Inc. Chestertown. 410-778-3300
Easton Memorial Hospital. 219 S. Washington Street. Easton. 410-822-1000
Dorchester General. 300 Byrn Street. Cambridge. 410-228-5511
Edward W. McCready Hospital. Hall Highway. Crisfield. 410-968-1200
Peninsula Regional Medical Center. 100 E. Carroll Street. Salisbury. 410-546-6400

Music

Pell Gardens. Chesapeake City. Summer evening concerts
Muskrat Park. St. Michael's. Thursday evening concerts
The Eastern Shore Chamber Music Festival. 410-819-0380

Theaters

Avalon Theater. Easton. 410-822-0345
Church Hill Theater. Centreville. 410-758-1331
Class Acts II. Salisbury. 410-742-6436
Pocomoke Players. Pocomoke City. 410-957-1919
Cecil Community College Cultural Center. North East. 410-287-1037
Tred Avon Players. Oxford Community Center

Yachting

See chapter on yachting

Golf Courses

Public Golf Courses:

Queenstown Harbor Golf Links. 310 Links Lane. Queenstown. 410-827-6611
Hunter's Oak Golf Course. 500 Amberly Farm Road. Queenstown. 410-827-0800
Blue Heron Golf Course. 3270 Romancoke Road. Stevensville. 410-643-0668
The Easton Club. 28449 Clubhouse Drive. Easton. 410-820-9800
Hog Neck Golf Course. 10142 Old Cordova Road. Easton. 410-822-6079
River Marsh Golf Club. Hyatt Regency Chesapeake Bay. 100 Heron Drive. Cambridge. 410-901-6396

Linkwood Family Golf Park. 37125 Linkwood Drive. Linkwood. 410-221-8700
Mears Great Oak Landing Golf Course. 22170 Great Oak Landing. Chestertown. 410-778-5007
Brantwood Golf Club. 1190 Augustine Highway. Elkton. 410-398-8848
Horse Bridge Golf Course. 32418 Mt. Hermon Road. Salisbury. 410-543-4446
Assateague Greens Golf Center. Rte. 611 and Eagle's Nest Road. Berlin. 410-213-7526
Bay Club – East & West. 9122 Liberty Road. Berlin. 410-641-4081
Eagle's Landing Golf Course. 12367 Eagle's Nest Road. Berlin. 410-213-7277
Peninsula Golf Center. 11004 Worcester Highway. Berlin. 410-641-5442
Pine Shore North. 11285 Beauchamp Road. Berlin. 410-641-5100
Pine Shore South. Rte. 611. Ocean City. 410-641-3300
River Run Golf Club & Community Golf Course. 11605 Master's Lane. Berlin. 410-641-7200
Rum Pointe Golf Course. 7000 Rum Pointe Lane. Berlin. 410-629-1414
Winter Quarters Golf Course. 355 Winter Quarters Drive. Pocomoke City. 410-957-1171
Great Hope Golf Course. 8380 Crisfield Highway. Westover. 410-651-5900
Nutters Crossing Golf Club & Driving Range. 30287 Southampton Bridge Road. Salisbury. 410-860-4653
Chesapeake Bay Golf Club. 1500 Chesapeake Club Drive. North East. 410-287-0200
Upland Golf Club. 23780 Thawley Road. Denton. 410-634-1200
Deer Run Golf Club. 8804 Logtown Road. Berlin. 410-629-0060
Elks Lodge Golf Course. 401 Churchill Avenue. Salisbury. 410-749-2695
Green Hill Yacht & Country Club. 5471 Whitehaven Road. Quantico. 410-749-1605
The Links at Lighthouse Sound. 12723 St. Martin's Neck Road. Bishopville. 410-352-5767
Ocean City Golf Club. 11401 Country Club Drive. Berlin. 410-641-1779
Ocean Pines Golf & Country Club. 100 Clubhouse Drive. Ocean Pines. 410-641-6057
Ocean Resorts Golf Club. 10655 Cathell Road. Berlin. 410-641-5643
Talbot Country Club. 6142 Country Club Drive. Easton. 410-822-0490
Wood Creek Golf Course. 9080 Executive Club Drive. Delmar. 410-896-3000

Semi-private:

The Beach Club Golf Links. 9715 Deer Park Drive. Berlin. 410-641-GOLF
Cambridge Country Club. 5670 Horn Point Road. Cambridge. 410-228-4808
Caroline County Club. 24820 Pealiquor Road. Denton. 410-479-2305
Harbourtowne Golf Resort & Conference Center. Martingham Drive, St. Michael's. 800-446-9066

Nassawango Golf Club. 3940 Nassawango Road. Snow Hill. 410-957-2262
Nutters Crossing Golf Club. 30287 Southampton Bridge Road. Salisbury. 410-860-4653
Ocean City Golf & Yacht Club. 11401 Country Club Road. Berlin. 800-442-3570

Private:

Chester River Yacht & Country Club. Quaker Neck Road. Chestertown. 410-778-1372
Cove Creek Country Club. 114 N. Creek Ct. Stevensville. 410-643-4868
Ocean Pines Golf & Country Club. 1449 Ocean Pines. Berlin. 410-641-8653
Prospect Bay Country Club. Prospect Bay Drive. Grasonville. 410-827-6924

Baseball

The Shorebirds play at Arthur W. Perdue Stadium, Salisbury. 410-219-3112. They are a farm team of the Baltimore Orioles. 410-685-9800

Bicycle Rentals and Sales

Happy Trails Bike Shop. Stevensville. 410-643-0670
Blackwater Paddle & Pedal. 4303 Bucktown Road. Cambridge. 410-901-9255
Mears Yacht Haven. Oxford. 410-266-5450
St. Michael's Town Dock Marina. 410-745-2400
St. Michael's Harbour Inn & Marina. 410-745-9001
Oxford Mews Bike Rentals & Repairs. 105 S. Morris Street, Oxford. 410-820-8222
Bikework. 208 S. Cross Street. Chestertown. 410-778-6940
Rock Hall Landing Marina. Hawthorne Avenue. Rock Hall. 410-639-2224
Easton Cycle & Sport. 723 Goldsborough Street. 410-822-7433
Swan Haven B&B. 20950 Rock Hall Avenue. Rock Hall. 410-639-2527
Bike Sport. 1013 S. Salisbury Blvd. Salisbury. 410-543-2453
Wheel Doctor. 1013 S. Talbot Street. St. Michael's. 410-745-6676
Bike Shop 523 Race Street. Cambridge. 410-228-7554
Easton Bike Shop. Rte. 50. 410-822-8580
Ol Reliable Rentals, Inc. Rte. 50 & Piney Hall Road. Trappe. 410-476-3055
Easton Cycle and Sport. 723 Goldsborough Street. Easton. 410-822-7433
Cambridge Cycle and Sport. 109 Cedar Street. Cambridge. 410-901-8380

Riding

Country Comfort Farm. St. Michael's. 410-745-3160
Crimson Stables. Rte. 291, Chestertown. 410-778-7304
Sassafras River Natural Resource Management Area. 410-778-1948
Nancy Cummings Riding School. Oxford. 410-822-3229
Windy Hill. Quaker Neck Road. Chestertown. 410-778-4346
Jewel's Landing. 410-634-1436
Hamilton Fox Farm. 410-749-6794
Frontier Town. Ocean City. 410-641-0057
Holly Ridge Equestrian Center. 410-835-2596
Hoof Prints in the Sand. 410-835-8814

Hunting

The Eastern Shore of Maryland has a number of Wildlife Management Areas (WMA) and other areas set aside for hunting. For more information contact the Maryland Department of Natural Resources.

Schrader's Hunting. 900 Red Lion Branch Road. Millington. 410-778-1895. Schrader's has over 10,000 acres for hunting deer, dove, mallard, quail, pheasant, chukar and sea ducks.
J&P Hunting Lodge. 1105 Benton Corner Road. Sudlersville. 410-438-3832. Sporting clay range, guided Upland Bird hunts
Native Shore Hunting Preserve. 621 Grange Hall Road. Centreville. 410-758-2428. Game hunts
Pintail Point. 511 Pintail Point Farm Lane. Queenstown. 410-827-7029. Released hunts
Quaker Neck Gun Club. Chestertown. 410-778-6965. Duck, whitetail deer and dove are offered here.
Great Goose Hunting. Rock Hall. 410-639-7619
Alexander Sporting Farms. Golts. 410-928-3549
B & J Guide Service. Chestertown. 410-928-5260
Fair Winds Gun Club. 5886 Quaker Neck Road. Chestertown. 410-778-5363
Sea Dux Outfitters. 115 Pintail Road. Chestertown. 410-778-4362. Duck
Hopkins Game Farm. Kennedyville. 410-348-5287. Pheasant, quail, chukar, Hungarian partridge, mallard, deer
Millington Wildlife Management Area. 410-928-3650
Loblolly Landings & Lodge. 2142 Liners Road. Church Creek. 410-397-3033. Spring turkey and deer
Delmarva Sporting Clays. 23501 Marsh Road. Mardela. 410-742-2023
The Woodlands Sporting Clays. 4633 Ocean Gateway. Vienna. 410-376-0200

E & M Farms. Church Creek. 410-228-2393
Florida Point Farms. 4710 Raven Wood Road. Vienna. 21869
Wayne Gatling Guide Service. 25046 E. Kentfield Road. Worton. 410-778-3191. Hunting and sportfishing
Tom Marvel. Outfitter. 13011 Ireland Corner Road. Galena. 410-648-5229. Duck, geese and deer hunts
South Chesapeake Gunning Club. Crisfield. 800-843-7918

Fishing

Chesapeake Bay, rivers and creeks
Goose Valley Fish Farms. Kennedyville. 410-778-5300
Millington Wildlife Management Area. 410-928-3650

Ice Skating

Carousel Hotel. 11700 Coastal Highway. Ocean City. 410-524-1000

Tennis

Cross Court Athletic Club. 5 Washington Street, Easton. 410-822-1515
Bay Country Racquet Club. 515 Leonard Lane, Cambridge. 410-476-5146
Layton's Salisbury Sports Club. Court Plaza, Salisbury. 410-749-6923

Parks/Wildlife Refuges

The Eastern Shore has a multitude of parks and wildlife management areas for hiking, picnicking, canoeing, bird watching and just to enjoy nature and its beauty.

Kent County:

Eastern Neck National Wildlife Refuge. Eastern Neck Road. Rock Hall
Chesapeake Farms Wildlife Habitat. 7319 Remington Drive. Chestertown
Betterton Beach. Rte 292. Beach
Millington Wildlife Management Area. Maryland-Line Road. Massey
Remington Farms. Chestertown. Private wildlife refuge
Rock Hall Town Beach. Beach Road
Turner's Creek and Sassafras River Natural Resource Management Area

Queen Anne's County:

Queen Anne's County offers a free map "Explore Our Great Outdoors".
Cross Island Trail. Crosses Kent Island
Adkins Arboretum. Eveland Road. Queen Anne
Chesapeake Bay Environmental Center. 600 Discovery Lane. Grasonville
Martinak State Park. 137 Deep Shore Road. Denton
Wye Island Natural Resources Management Area. 632 Wye Island road. Queenstown
Upper Tuckahoe Creek and Tuckahoe State Park. Queen Anne
Adkins Arboretum. Tuckahoe State Park
Terrapin Nature Area
Cross Island Trail. Stevensville to Chester

Cecil County:

Stemmers Run Wildlife Management Area
Earleville W.M.A.
Courthouse Point W.M.A.
Elk Neck Forest. Irishtown Road. North East
Elk Neck State Park. North East.

Talbot County:

Pickering Creek Environmental Center. Easton
Wye Oak State Park. Wye Mills
Seth State Forest
Third Haven Woods Wildlife Preserve
Choptank River Fishing Pier. Rte. 50 near Cambridge

Somerset County:

Janes Island State Park. Crisfield
Martin's National Wildlife Refuge Visitor's Center. Caleb Jones Road. Ewell
William B. Mullins Education Center. Chesapeake Bay Foundation. 21151 Marshall Street. Tylerton
Deal Island Wildlife Management Area. 10,000 acre wildlife area on Deal Island
Cedar Island Wildlife Management Area. South of Byrdtown
South Marsh Island Wildlife Management Area
Fairmount Wildlife Management Area
Wellington Wildlife Management Area
Pocomoke River State Forest
Pocomoke Sound Wildlife Management Area

Dorchester County:

Blackwater National Wildlife Refuge
Martinak State Park and Watts Creek. Denton
Long Wharf Park and Pier. Cambridge. Summer concerts
Sailwinds Park. 200 Byrn Street. Cambridge.
LeCompte Wildlife Management Area
Taylor's Island Wildlife Management Area
Linkwood Wildlife Management Area

Worcester County:

Pocomoke River State Forest and Park, Rte. 113. 12,000 acre of property that had been abandoned by farmers because of depleted soil. During the Civil War it may have been part of the Underground Railroad
Shad Landing State Park
Milburn Landing State Park. River Road. Camping, fishing, picnicking and walking.
Cypress Park, Pocomoke City – boat dock, ball field, tennis courts
Pocomoke City Nature and Exercise Trail, Cypress Park
Beach to Bay Indian Trail
Pocomoke Cypress Swamp, Hickory Point Road
Assateague Island National Seashore. Berlin
Assateague State Park. Berlin
Goat Island Nature Trail. Snow Hill
E. A. Vaughn W.M.A.

Wicomico County:

Wicomico Demonstration Forest
Ellis Bay W.M.A.
Johnson W.M.A.

Caroline County:

Idylwild Wildlife Management Area. Federalsburg. This 3,000 acre area has walking trails along the Marshyhope Creek.

Zoos

Salisbury Zoological Park. 750 S. Park Drive, Salisbury

Colleges and Universities

Washington College. Washington Avenue. 410-778-2800
Chesapeake College. Wye Mills. 410-822-5400
Chesapeake College. Race Street. Cambridge. 410-228-5754
Salisbury State University. 1101 Camden Avenue. Salisbury. 410-543-6030
University of Maryland Eastern Shore. Princess Anne. 410-651-2200
Wor-Wic Community College. 3200 Campus Drive. Salisbury. 410-334-2800
University of Maryland Center for Environmental Science. Cambridge. 410-228-9250

Private Schools/Special Schools

Gunston Day School. Centreville. 410-758-0620
St. Andrew's School. Middletown, DE. Though not on Maryland's Eastern Shore this nearby school has attracted many Eastern Shore students.
Kent School. Chestertown. 410-778-4100. PreK-8th grade
St. Peter & Paul School. High and Choptank Avenue. Easton. 410-822-2275. Grades 9-12
Country School. 716 Goldsborough Street. Easton. 410-822-1935. K-8th grade
Echo Hill Outdoor School. 13655 Bloomingneck Road. Worton. 410-348-5880. Offers students programs in science and ecology, history and the environment, and group and individual development.

Special Libraries

Geddes - Piper House. Chestertown. Genealogical records, historic site surveys
Howard I. Chappelle Memorial Library. Chesapeake Bay Maritime Museum. St. Michael's. Information about the Chesapeake and writings of Mr. Chappelle, a boat builder
Talbot County Free Library. Easton. Research facility that was used by James Michener to write "Chesapeake".
Salisbury State University Research Center for Delmarva History and Culture. In Holloway Hall. 410-543-6246

How to Make it on the Eastern Shore

Dressing the Part

Dress is very important on the Eastern Shore. It is basically a casual region. However appropriate dress is advised. Ladies should not be seen in short shorts, low cut dresses or bathing suits.

Men should not wear tank tops, tee shirts, short shorts, or be bare chested. No bathing suits except at the beach.

Men

Daytime:
Khaki pants or shorts
Polo shirts
Topsiders
No socks
Foul weather gear

Evening Wear: Some restaurants and yacht clubs require coat and tie. For yacht christenings and special events navy blue blazer, tan or white pants, club or regimental tie.

Ladies

Daytime:
Khaki, linen or silk pants
Shorts
Polo shirt
Blazers or wool sweaters
Topsiders

Evening Wear: Nice dress - silk or cotton. Silk pants and blouse.

Talking the Part

There are a number of variations of English on the Eastern Shore. One only has to travel to Smith Island to hear something like "Elizabethan English". The watermen have their own way of speaking. And then there are the old line wealthy families, many whom have moved here from Wilmington and Philadelphia, that still talk in "Main Line Lockjaw". Sometimes it's a bit of a strain to understand any of them!!!

Where to take your favorite girl or beau

Breakfast H&G, Easton

Sunday Brunch	208 Talbot Street, St. Michael's Imperial Hotel, Chestertown
Lunch	The Bayard House, Chesapeake City;
Tea	White Swan Tavern, Chestertown;
Drinks	Carpenter Street, St. Michael's;
Dinner	The Inn at Perry Cabin, St. Michael's; Inn at Osprey Point, Rock Hall
Seafood	Robert Morris Inn, Oxford; Town Dock, St. Michael's; The Narrows, Grasonville; Crab Claw, St. Michael's; Fisherman's Wharf; Grasonville; Harris', Kent Narrows
Music	Evening concerts on the town greens Big band concerts, St. Michael's Summer evening concerts
Sightseeing	Anywhere on the Eastern Shore
Drive	Rte.213
Sailing	Anywhere on Bay, rivers or creeks

Things to do on a great day

Go sailing, canoeing, or kayaking
Learn to sail
Watch the sailboats
Girl watch on the harbors
Sit at one of the outdoor cafes and people watch
Take a walking tour of any of the historic towns
Take a picnic to the Bay or along one of the rivers – the ferry beach at Oxford is lovely. You can even ride the ferry from Oxford to Bellevue
Walk in a park or around some of the towns' historic squares or one of the nature preserves
Visit the Chesapeake Bay Maritime Museum
Take a bicycle ride
Take a balloon ride
Charter a fishing boat
Eat an ice cream cone
Go crabbing
Buy a boat

Things to Do on a Rainy Day

Find the best crab cakes
Go to a museum

Go to the movies
Sit in a bar, meet new friends and be patient. Just don't get drunk as Maryland has strict DWI laws.
Go antique shopping

Things to do for free on a Summer Evening

Evening concerts at the local bandstand
Wednesday night sail boat races
Watch the sunset every evening
Watch the sunset every evening from your own boat

Things to do for Free on a Winter Evening

Curl up in front of a fire with a good book
Hang out at one of the local pubs (you will have to purchase a drink or two, but you'll get some lively conversation)
Listen to some good music
Go to a lecture

Favorite Pets

Black, yellow and chocolate Labradors, and Chesapeakes (Chessies) are favorite pets, and are also used for hunting.

The Best of the Eastern Shore

Special Places to Stay with the Best View

Sometimes you might want to get away for a night or a week-end. These places are recommended for that special occasion.

Wade's Point Inn. St. Michael's
Inn at Perry Cabin, St. Michael's
Kent Manor Inn & Restaurant. Stevensville
Lands End Manor on the Bay. Grasonville

Other Special Places to Stay

Merry Sherwood Plantation, Berlin
White Swan Inn, Chestertown
Waterloo. Princess Anne
Robert Morris Inn. Oxford

Special Meeting Facilities

The Aspen Institute. Wye River Conference Center. Queenstown
The Tidewater Inn & Conference Center. Easton
The Oaks Lodging & Conference Center. Royal Oak
Harbourtown Golf Resort & Conference Center. St. Michael's
Hyatt Regency. 100 Heron Boulevard. Cambridge

Restaurants to Arrive by Boat

Tilghman Island Inn. Tilghman Island
Bay Hundred. Tilghman Island
Inn at Perry Cabin. St. Michael's
Crab Claw. St. Michael's
Old Wharf. Chestertown
Town Dock. St. Michael's
Harrison's. Tilghman Island
The Narrows. Kent Island
Fisherman's Inn. Kent Island
Harris'. Kent Island
Robert Morris Inn. Oxford

The Best Place to Watch a Sunset

Anywhere along the shores of the Bay since it faces west. The Wade's Point Inn, St. Michael's, has one of the most spectacular views to the west, north and even east up the Miles River. Sunrises on the harbors can be just as lovely so rise early to watch this.

Wye Mills, Wye Mills c1682

Chapter 2

Eastern Shore History

The Bay was formed about 15,000 years ago by glaciers in the Susquehanna Valley. The earliest inhabitants of the Chesapeake area were wanderers that began to settle c 1,000 BC. The creation of the bow and arrow c 500 AD and the cultivation of crops c 800 AD led to permanent villages. The Algonquin were the predominant group with the Susquehannocks just to the north. Most of the food came from the Chesapeake Bay - fish, especially rockfish and shad, crabs, oysters and the fertile land produced an abundance of crops.

The earliest white man to enter the Chesapeake Bay was Giovanni da Verrazano in 1524 who sailed on the *Dauphine* and landed in Worcester County, calling the land Arcadia. He explored some of the Eastern Shore, but turned back at the marshes of the Pocomoke River. Bartholomew Gilbert, while looking for Sir Walter Raleigh's colony was driven into the bay in a storm in 1603. He sailed north and probably came into Bullock's Channel between Smith's Island and the Eastern Shore.

The earliest English explorer of the Chesapeake Bay was Captain John Smith who set out in 1608 from Jamestown. He made a second trip and sailed to the Tockwogh, or Sassafras River. Tockwogh is a variation of Tuckahoe, a root. He also entered the Chester River. He was provided the first detailed map of the Chesapeake Bay region.

William Claiborne, who had been appointed secretary of state in Virginia by King Charles I, was commissioned in 1625 to discover the source of the Chesapeake Bay. He also obtained a license to trade with the Indians. He established a trading post on Kent Island, just across from present day Annapolis in 1631. By 1634 approximately 100 lived in this settlement. The first boat, the *Long Tayle*, built in Maryland was for Mr. Claiborne. The location of this settlement is thought to be Kent Fort Manor which is marked with a stone marker today.

George Calvert, the first Lord Baltimore, was given a grant in 1632 from King Charles I for all the land between the 40th parallel and the low water mark of the Potomac River to its source. He had hoped to found a colony in America, but only got as far as Newfoundland and found the area too cold and abandoned his project. A second grant (probably 10-12 million acres) was given to his son Cecil Calvert, a Catholic, who left Virginia, which was an Anglican settlement. His wife, Anne Arundel, was the daughter of Lord Wardour. His brothers

Leonard and George founded Maryland after sailing aboard the "Ark" and "Dove" with 140 passengers and landing at St. Clement's Island in the Potomac. He arrived in 1634 meeting with the Piscataway Indians, and bought a village, later St. Mary's City, and became the first Colonial Governor. As Lord Baltimore he could raise an army, incorporate towns, impose duties, establish courts, appoint government officials and vest titles. In return he gave the king 2 Indian arrows every Easter, and 1/5 of the precious metals mined in the colony. In Lord Baltimore's patent Watkins Point was the southernmost point on the Eastern Shore. This was at the north side of the entrance to Pocomoke Sound.

Because the charter given to Lord Baltimore was for "uncultivated" land, William Claiborne argued that his settlement was cultivated. Governor Calvert was later to seize Kent Island in the first battle in the American colonies. George Evelin was made commander of Kent Island and given a manor. By 1638 Kent Island became the second county in Maryland and sent delegates to the Maryland Assembly.

The Calverts began granting land in what is now Talbot County in 1649. In 1661 Governor Calvert appointed a commission for the Eastern Shore to make grants of land south of the Choptank River. One of the earliest writers about Maryland and the Eastern Shore was George Alsop who wrote *Character of the Province of Maryland* in 1666.

In 1658 Lord Baltimore granted Col. Henry as much land as he could cover with his thumb on a map for his role in negotiating peace with the Indians. Most of that surrounded Queenstown in Queen Anne County.

The first court house for Kent County was located in New Yarmouth, south of what is now known as Rock Hall. In 1674 Charles Calvert ordered the removal of court sessions from Eastern Neck Island. The court later moved to New Town (now Chestertown).

The main settlers on the Eastern Shore were English, but in the 1680s Scotch-Irish families also arrived. Unlike most of the other settlers, who were Anglican or Roman Catholics, the Scotch-Irish were Presbyterians. Among the settlers was the Dennis family who lived at Beverly of Worcester on the Pocomoke River. A descendent of the family John Upshur, traded Pocomoke cypress for molasses in the West Indies. Francis Jenckins also lived on the Pocomoke and married Mary, daughter of Sir Robert King of Ireland. After her husband's death she married John Henry, pastor of Rehoboth Church.

An early explorer of the region was George Talbot from Roscommon County, Ireland. He received in 1680 a patent to Susquehanna Manor, a 32,000-acre estate that extended from the Northeast River ten miles up to the Susquehanna.

Another large landowner was Augustine Herman, who arrived from Prague via New Amsterdam, and owned over 20,000 acres on the Eastern Shore granted by Lord Baltimore. The Bohemia River flows through this grant which is known as Bohemia Manor. He published a map of the area in 1674. This extended the boundaries of Lord Baltimore's properties to include most of the Delaware River. William Penn lay claim on some of this. The matter was not settled until the Mason-Dixon Line was established in 1767. Mr. Herman also drew up plans for a canal, that did not materialize until the Chesapeake and Delaware Canal was completed in 1829. Part of Bohemia Manor was sold to a sect called the Labadists from Holland, led by Peter Sluyter. Nothing remains of the group today except for historical markers.

A number of Quakers also settled on the Eastern Shore on the Annemessex River. Stephen Horsey led the group from Accomac, Virginia. He had been thrown out of the Virginia Assembly for insisting on his rights. He was also one of the six signers of the Northampton Protest that raised the question of taxation without representation. But it was his refusal to pay tithes to the Church of England that led to his settling in a more religious-tolerant Maryland.

The governor of Maryland, Cecil Calvert, empowered three men to grant land warrants and administer the oath of allegiance to the colonists. One of the three chosen was Charles Scarborough, who sought however to protect Virginia's interests on the Eastern Shore of Virginia. Mr. Scarborough, the court physician to King Charles II, had immigrated to Virginia. He punished Quakers and made the colonists in Somerset pay taxes to Virginia. He later was to own several large estates.

The main occupation of landowners was growing tobacco. The tobacco cash crop was used to support the clergy and churches and 40 pounds of tobacco was levied per taxable inhabitant. Many slaves and indentured servants came to work for the tobacco planters. Large plantations were built along the Wye and Chester Rivers. Tobacco was used as money. In the areas of the Eastern Shore that were swamplands or had poor soil, shipbuilding or other uses of lumber products developed.

Not only were there blacks slaves, but white servants could also be bought and sold. A number of convicts were sent to Maryland in 1633-80 and 1746-75, some coming to the Eastern Shore. However, the population of the Eastern Shore grew very slowly, and had few women. By 1707 there were about 2,000 black slaves on the Eastern Shore out of a population of 3,000. By 1755 there would be approximately 17,000 slaves.

One of the first Eastern Shore farmers to switch from growing tobacco to wheat farming was John Beale Bordley of Wye Island. Mr. Bordley's brother-in-law was William Paca of Wye Narrows and Annapolis. William Paca studied law under Stephen Bordley, brother of John. They along with the Lloyd family were to become some of the wealthiest families on the Eastern Shore and in Maryland.

The population of the Eastern Shore increased to 15,000 by 1760. Prior to the revolutionary War, Maryland had supported the Tobacco Inspection Act to maintain high quality tobacco for export. However, the Upper and Lower Houses of the Assembly failed to agree on the new act when the Tobacco Inspection Act of 1747 was to end in 1770. The Lower House warned public officials and clergy not to accept further fees. William Stewart, clerk of the Land Office, was arrested for ignoring the warning. Governor Eden dismissed the Assembly, and then freed William Stewart. He then issued the Fee Proclamation on November 26, 1770 which allowed public officials and clergy to continue collecting their tobacco fee. The Lower House demanded its repeal. Finally after much public protest, the Assembly passed a new Tobacco Inspection Act in 1773 that had no fee bill.

Also in 1773 the British Parliament passed the Tea Act that allowed the East India Company to undersell all other companies in the American market. Massachusetts's citizens reacted by staging the Boston Tea Party in December 1773. The British closed Boston as a port. Opposition to the British began to grow in all the colonies. Chestertown had its own Tea Party on May 23, 1774 when Chestertown citizens boarded a British ship, the brigantine *Geddes* and dumped its cargo of tea.

A convention of 92 delegates met in Annapolis on June 22, 1774 and elected Matthew Tilghman chairman. By August of 1775 five conventions had been held. In December 1775 and May 1776 the Maryland delegates to the Continental Congress were instructed not to vote for independence. The number of British troops increased in the colonies and British vessels entered the Chesapeake Bay.

In June 1776 Maryland sent 2,000 men to fight for the Continental Army. Governor Eden remained in the Maryland colony until that month. On June 28 the Maryland Convention unanimously adopted a resolution to allow its delegates to the Congress to support independence. Matthew Tilghman was one of those leading the argument. Four signers of the Declaration of Independence were from Maryland – Charles Carroll of Carrollton, William Paca, Samuel Chase and Thomas Stone. Samuel Chase was born near Princess Anne in 1741. He was appointed to the Supreme Court in 1796 where he remained until his death in 1811.

During the Revolutionary War Maryland suffered difficult economic times. Wheat replaced tobacco as the main agricultural product. But the shipbuilding business became ever more important.

Following the war the new state constitution gave more power to the Maryland counties. The Upper House of the Assembly, the Senate, was made up of 9 members from the Western Shore and 6 from the Eastern Shore. There were also two states offices, one for the Western Shore, located in Annapolis and one for the Eastern Shore in Easton.

In the early 1800s the United States needed foreign commerce, but had a problem with British ships entering the Chesapeake. In 1807 the British ship Leopard took the frigate *Chesapeake* at the mouth of the Chesapeake. The British boarded and impressed 4 sailors. Embargoes on trade were declared in 1794 and 1807, with war finally declared by President James Madison in 1812. Many of the Eastern Shore towns were attacked as the British pushed their way towards Washington. These included:

St. Michael's – 1813, but saved by the ingenuous citizens who rigged lanterns in trees and masts, and only one cannonball hit any building
Kent Island, which was occupied by the British in 1813
Queenstown – attacked 1813
Battle of Caulk's Field - 1814
Georgetown – burned 1813

After the War of 1812 a number of people from the Eastern Shore settled in other regions of the state where the soil was more fertile. For those that stayed many freed their slaves. Towns that had been depended on as ports fell victim to the growth of Baltimore as the major port in the region. Towns such as Oxford which had shipped large amounts of tobacco had to find other means of commerce. St. Michael's grew in prominence as a shipbuilding center. Easton flourished as the administrative center for the Eastern Shore.

Besides agriculture, harvesting of the Chesapeake Bay took a prominent role. Oysters were shipped to Baltimore and Philadelphia. The opening of the Chesapeake and Delaware Canal in 1829 allowed produce and seafood to be transported north more quickly.

From 1830-50 the Eastern Shore of Maryland attempted to secede from Maryland. The question also came up that perhaps the Eastern Shore should become one state with the Delaware, Maryland and Virginia regions. This was initiated by Delaware, but the Senate voted it down. In the election of 1860 Abraham Lincoln received only 2% of the Maryland vote. When seven states proclaimed themselves the Confederate States of America in February 1861,

Maryland lost all of its trade with the South. Two days after the Confederacy began firing on federal property at Fort Sumter President Lincoln called for 75,000 volunteers to put down the insurrection. Many Marylanders volunteered, but one group opposed Northern troops passing through Maryland. A bloody riot broke out in Baltimore in April 1861 due to this. Maryland was to remain in the Union, and elected a pro-Union governor in 1861, Augustus Bradford.

A small number of Marylanders, mainly from the Eastern Shore, did join the Confederacy. Edward Long and James Upshur Dennis, both members of the House of Delegates and from the Eastern Shore, were slave owners and promoted the Confederate cause. James Crisfield, also a slave owner, however, did go to Washington to try to prevent the war in February 1861 and remained loyal to the Union. In the census of 1860, there were 24,957 slaves and 28,277 free blacks in the Eastern Shore counties. Some of these blacks were to serve on both sides in the military during the war. Those enlisting in the Union Army joined the 9th and 19th Colored Troops of Maryland. Isaiah "Uncle Zear" Fassett was one of those to serve in many battles and was to attend the 75th Battle Reunion at Gettysburg in 1938.

Some Eastern Shore families were Methodists who advocated against slavery. Frederick Douglass, born on one of the Lloyd plantations was an early abolitionist. The Eastern Shore was part of the Underground Railroad, led by Harriet Tubman. After the war many blacks founded Methodist churches, or joined the Baptist Church. They started communities such as Brownsville near Centreville, but had very few schools. The first secondary school for African Americans in Queen Anne's County was not founded until 1936 at the Kennard School.

Following the Civil War, trains and steamships opened up the Eastern Shore to travelers. Resorts were established at Tolchester and Betterton. Farmers began to diversify their crops and grew corn, potatoes, melons, tomatoes, berries, peaches, and wheat. The steamboats and trains could carry this produce to a variety of markets including Baltimore, Philadelphia and even New York. Canneries processed seafood, and refrigerated cars allowed shipments throughout the country. John Woodland Crisfield, a U.S. Congressman and President of the Eastern Shore Railroad connected Somers Cove (now Crisfield) with Philadelphia by railroad. Crisfield became the largest oyster center in the state by 1872.

Both Marylanders and Virginians vied for valuable oyster beds leading to the Oyster Wars of the Chesapeake Bay. In 1877 under the Jenkins Award, Maryland gave up 23,000 acres of oyster beds to Virginia. The Maryland General Assembly created the Oyster Navy to control these rivalries. By 1885 the oyster beds were beginning to be depleted. Dredging for the remaining oysters led to increased rivalries and unlicensed dredging. In 1886 the Maryland state steamer *McLane*, enforcing state law, fought a battle with several illegal dredgers, sinking two schooners and capturing several others. On January 2, 1889 the Maryland state steamer *Helen Baughman* fought another battle with the unlicensed dredging schooner *Robert McAllister.* The rivers and Chesapeake Bay froze during the winter of 1917-18 and trucks could drive over the surface. On Tilghman Island holes were dug in the ice to get the oysters.

During World War II German POWs were brought to the United States. The War Department in Washington informed the state of Maryland that several camps would be located in the state. The largest was located at Ft. Meade. By 1945 over 3,000 prisoners were in camps on the Eastern Shore, including Camp Somerset, five miles south of Princess Anne. During 1944-45 the POWs worked as contract laborers for the local farmers, in the canneries, orchards and sawmills in Princess Anne and Salisbury. After the war the camp was converted into a migrant labor camp.

A major change came to the Eastern Shore in 1952 when the William Preston Lane Memorial Bridge was opened, connecting the Eastern and Western Shores. Construction had begun in 1949 when Governor William Preston Lane introduced a 2% sales tax. The bridge cost $112 million to build. This allowed visitors to get quickly to the Eastern Shore and Maryland and Delaware beaches.

The Eastern Shore continued to increase production of agricultural crops, but the raising of chickens also became important. Perdue, Allen and Tyson chickens were to become household names.

Desegregation in Maryland began in 1948. On June 11, 1963 riots took place, later to be quelled only with the arrival of the National Guard in Cambridge. In that year a new state law prohibited discrimination in hotels, restaurants and other public places. However, the Eastern Shore was exempted from this. Sit-ins and demonstrations continued to take place.

Today the Eastern Shore faces even more of a challenge – too much growth in population and building. Large farms are being broken up and whole new communities built. The oyster and crab population too, is depleted. Yet even so, the Eastern Shore remains a vibrant, historic region that is truly a national treasure.

Famous Eastern Shore People

Tench Tilghman – aide-de-camp to George Washington during the Revolutionary War. Col. Tilghman was born at Fausley near Easton in 1744, and moved with his father James to Philadelphia in 1762. He became a well-to-do merchant. During the war his father remained a loyalist, but Col. Tilghman supported the Americans. He became George Washington's secretary and later aide-de-camp. When the victory came at Yorktown, Col. Tilghman carried the news to the Continental congress in Philadelphia. He later went into business with Robert Morris. His wife was Anna Maria Tilghman, daughter of Matthew Tilghman.

Matthew Tilghman – was the son of Richard Tilghman of Queen Anne's County. In 1741 he married Ann Lloyd. He served as justice of the peace for Talbot County, represented Talbot County in the General Assembly from 1751-57, and later was speaker of the house. He served as president of the provincial convention in 1776 and was chairman of the committee that drafted the constitution of Maryland.

Frederick Douglas - was born into slavery in 1818 on Holmes Farm near Easton, owned by Aaron Anthony, a former ship's captain and manager of a plantation owned by Edward Lloyd V. He spent his early years working on the plantation of Edward Lloyd V, where he went to live with his grandmother, Betsey Bailey, a slave. At the age of nine he was sent to be a companion to the son of some Lloyd relatives, the Auld's in Baltimore. The mother taught him the alphabet, which was a violation of keeping slaves ignorant. When the son was in school Mr. Douglas worked in a shipyard and eventually became a caulker. He was to learn about abolition in 1831. In 1838 he escaped from slavery by disguising himself as a sailor and fleeing to Philadelphia. He became a free man and from then on, worked as a leading abolitionist. He died in 1895 and is buried in Rochester, New York. His home, Cedar Hill, is in the Anacostia section of Washington, D.C.

Harriet Tubman – was born as a slave in Dorchester County in about 1821. She married John Tubman, a free slave in the 1840s. She escaped to the north in 1849 and with the help of the Quakers and other abolitionists became active in the antislavery cause. She was involved the Underground Railroad as many slaves escaped via the Eastern Shore. During the Civil War she served as a spy for the Union Army in South Carolina. She died in Auburn, New York in 1913.

Rev. Dr. Charles Albert Tindley – was born in Berlin around 1855. He came from a slave family, but was able to educate himself for the ministry. He went on to found one of the largest African-American Methodist congregations in Philadelphia. He wrote a number of hymns, including "Songs of Paradise".

Charles Willson Peale – was born near Chestertown in 1741. He and his son, Rembrandt Peale, were good friends of George Washington, and painted a number of pictures of him. Charles Peale, father of Charles Willson Peale, was headmaster of the Kent County Free School from 1742-49.

Ezekiel Foreman Chambers – who lived in Chestertown, was a U.S. Senator and wrote legislation to found the Smithsonian Institution.

The Lloyd Family – The Lloyds lived on Wye Island beginning with Edward Lloyd in 1664. He had come from England. His son Philemon married Henrietta Maria Bennett. Philemon's son, Edward II served as acting Governor of Maryland from 1709-1714. Edward IV, known as "the patriot", was a member of the first Council of Safety, a delegate to the Continental Congress and a member of the Maryland Senate. Edward V served as Governor of Maryland in 1809 and U.S. Senator from 1819-26. His son-in-law was Franklin Buchanan, the first Superintendent at the U.S. Naval Academy. Another son-in-law was Isaac R. Trimble, a Confederate general. Edward V's grandson, Charles S. Winder, a Confederate brigade commander, was killed at the Battle of Cedar Mountain in 1862. The Lloyd's were the largest slave owners on the Eastern Shore.

Robert Morris – Robert Morris was the son of Robert Morris Senior who came to Oxford in 1738 as a factor for Foster Cunliffe, Esq. and Sons of Liverpool. Robert Morris Junior came to Oxford at about age 13, and then entered the Greenway countinghouse in Philadelphia. When Congress established a navy in 1775 Mr. Morris was named the first Secretary of the Navy. He was to become one of the wealthiest men in the colonies. He was one of two men (the other was Roger Sherman) to be a Signer of the Declaration of Independence, the Articles of Confederation, and the U.S. Constitution. He served as Finance Minister for the Confederation. He raised money for the Revolutionary War, using some of his own finances. He served as U.S. Senator from Pennsylvania. Unfortunately he lost his fortune and spent three years in debtor's prison.

James Alfred Pearce – also a U.S. Senator, prevented President Andrew Jackson from being impeached with his "No" Vote in 1868.

James Emory "Jimmie" Foxx – was born in Sudlersville in 1907. He played baseball for the Easton minor league team and then began a major league career. (See Sudlersville)

Bill Nicholson - was the first athlete honored with a statue in Maryland in Chestertown. In 1943 and 1944 he led the National League in home runs and RBIs. In 1944 he missed out on the MVP trophy by one vote to the St. Louis Cardinals shortstop Marty Marion. However that year he hit 33 home runs and drove in 122 runs. Mr. Nicholson was born in Chestertown in 1914 and died in

1996. He was a graduate of Washington College., and applied to the US. Naval Academy but was turned down for being color-blind.

Wayne Gilchrest - once taught citizenship at Kent County High School. Now U.S. Congressman from Maryland.

James Wallace - a Dorchester county lawyer, was asked by Gov. Thomas H. Hicks to raise and command the 1st Maryland Shore Volunteer Infantry during the Civil War. The unit served in the 12th Corps, Army of the Potomac and fought at the Battle of Gettysburg, fighting against Confederate Maryland troops at Culp's Hill. Mr. Wallace also owned canneries in Cambridge.

John Barth – was born in 1930 in Cambridge. His first novel, *The Floating Opera*, written in 1955, contains descriptions of Cambridge.

James Michener – author of many 20th c famous books lived in St. Michael's while writing *Chesapeake Bay.*

The duPont family – many members of the DuPont family settled on the Eastern Shore. Thomas Coleman DuPont, a U.S. Senator developed Horn Point in Cambridge. Francis P. DuPont donated this land to the city. The DuPonts have given thousands of acres of land for conservation on the Eastern Shore and are still involved in many activities here.

The King family- Robert King settled in Somerset County near King's Creek in 1682. He built a home called "Kingsland". His son, Robert II, acquired much wealth and many slaves. A grandson, Nehemiah King II, inherited "Kingsland" and built "Beverly" near Princess Anne in 1796. Thomas King, another grandson, was to build "Kingston Hall" on the Annemessex River. Thomas King Carroll, grandson of Thomas King became governor of Maryland. His daughter, Anna Ella Carroll became an activist and eventually wrote *Reply to Breckenridge*, in which she accused Southern leaders of threatening to secede as early as 1850.

James Wesley Nelson – who founded the Del Monte Company in California, was born in Crisfield.

Commodore Stephen Decatur - was born in Berlin in 1779. His father was a Revolutionary War naval officer who sent his wife to a farm in Maryland for safety when she had the baby. After four months she returned to Philadelphia. Comm. Decatur entered the Navy as a midshipman in 1798. From 1804-05 he fought against pirates in the Mediterranean and the British during the War of 1812. He was killed during a duel in Bladensburg, and is buried in Philadelphia.

Perdue family – owner of Perdue Farms, Inc. This was founded by Franklin Perdue. His son, Frank, left Salisbury State University in the 1930's to join his father. James Perdue now runs the poultry business in Salisbury.

Samuel Chase - was from Somerset County. He was a Signer of the Declaration of Independence and later Chief Justice of the United States.

Luther Martin – was a teacher in Somerset County and later Attorney General of Maryland. He was a staunch Federalist who opposed the views of Thomas Jefferson.

Ebenezer Cooke – was a poet whose father owned property at Cook Point at the mouth of the Choptank River. Cooke signed a petition against removing the Maryland capital from St. Mary's to Annapolis. He was also a tobacco trader, and lawyer, but is best known for his poetry. "The Sot Weed Factor or A Voyage to Maryland" was written in 1708 and "Sot Weed Redivius or the Planter Looking Glass" in 1730.

Sophie Kerr - Each year Washington College gives the Sophie Kerr Literary Prize for excellence in writing to a senior. This is the largest prize of its kind. Sophie Kerr was a writer who left the Eastern Shore (Denton) for New York. She wrote twenty novels, plays, magazine articles, and light essays.

Joshua Thomas – was born in 1776 and later became known as "Parson of the Islands". As a Methodist preacher he went about the Chesapeake in his boat *The Methodist.* During the War of 1812 the British rested on Tangier Island waiting to attack Baltimore. As they were departing the commander asked Joshua Thomas to preach to them. Holding his Bible he preached on repentance and the fact that all men are sinners. He told them God loved sinners, but they had to repent and then meet their final judge. God had warned Rev. Thomas that the British would not take Baltimore and many would perish. This truly happened and the British of course did not take Baltimore. Later Rev. Thomas moved to Devil's Island, which later was to be named Deal Island.

Francis Makemie – was born in Scotland, ordained a Presbyterian minister and was brought to Somerset County in the late 1600s by Judge William Stevens. Mr. Makemie constructed a meetinghouse on the judge's plantation on the Pocomoke River and later was instrumental in founding Presbyterian churches on the Eastern Shore. He is known as the "Father of Organized Presbytery in America".

Governors of Maryland from the Eastern Shore

1797-1798	John Henry – Dorchester County
1806-1809	Robert Wright – Queen Anne's County
1809-11	Edward Lloyd - Talbot County
1812-1816	Levin Winder – Somerset County
1819	Charles Goldsborough - Dorchester County
1822-26	Samuel Stevens, Jr. – Talbot County
1829-30	Daniel Martin – Talbot County
1839-42	William Grason – Queen Anne's County
1848-51	Philip Francis Thomas – Talbot County
1858-1862	Thomas Hicks – born 1798, farmer from Dorchester County, later appointed U.S. Senator
1885-88	Henry Lloyd – Dorchester County
1888-92	Elihu E. Jackson – Somerset County
1912-16	Phillips Lee Goldsborough – Cambridge
1916-20	Emerson C. Harrington – Dorchester County
1959-67	J. Millard Tawes – Somerset County
1979-86	Harry Hughes – Talbot County, born in Easton, but grew up in Denton

Silversmiths

The Bruff family
Richard Bruff. Talbot County. c1670-1730
Richard Bruff. Easton. c 1785
Thomas Bruff. Talbot County. c1648-1702
Thomas Bruff. Easton, Chestertown. 1760-1803
Charles Oliver Bruff. Easton. 1760-87
James Earle Bruff. Queen Anne's County. B c1710-80
Joseph Bruff. Easton. b c1730-85
Joseph J. Bruff. Easton, Chestertown. B c1770-1803

Bowdle & Needles. Easton.
William Needles. 1798-1818
James Bowdle

Lynch & Leonard
Chestertown? 1805

Edward Bradshaw. b 1787. Apprenticed to Benjamin Skinner, silversmith of Talbot County

Benjamin Skinner. Easton. 1801-03

John J. Clark. Cambridge. C1833

Edward Corner. Easton. b c1788

Stephen Hussey. Easton. 1818-30. Took over the shop of William Needles

Israel Johnson. Easton. 1793

Robert Smith. Easton. Jeweler. 1867

Furniture Makers

Easton provided a number of prominent furniture makers in the early 1800s. These included Tristam Needles, James and Joseph Neale, Thomas and Samuel Wainwright, Henry Bowdle, Thomas Meconokin and Jonathan Ozmet. John Shaw, a well-known Annapolis furniture maker provided much of the furniture for Wye House.

Clock and Watchmakers

Jonathan Benny. Easton. C1800
William Mullikin, Jr. Cambridge. 1823
James Murdock. Easton. 1815
James Troth. Easton. B 1782
Benjamin Willmott. Easton. 1797-1822
Nathan Downes. b 1785 apprenticed to Benjamin Willmott of Talbot County
Henry Jones. Easton. b 1799 apprenticed to James Ninde
William L. Jones. Easton 1834. Centreville c1837
Dominic Kinsley apprenticed 1775 to Elisha Winters of Kent County
Peter Kirkwood. Chestertown. 1790-95
John M. Laws. Easton. 1824

Did You Know?

Queen Anne's County was named for Queen Anne, daughter of King George II of England. She was born in 1665 and ascended the throne in 1702. The county was established in 1706 with Queenstown as the first county seat.

The Chester River meets the Bay at Eastern Neck Island. The headwaters are located in Delaware. The main part of the river is 60 miles long with 43 tributaries.

Somerset County is named for Mary Somerset, sister-in-law of Cecil Calvert, the 2nd Lord Baltimore. The county was established in 1666 to serve the Quakers, Presbyterians and other colonists who came from Virginia. The county motto is "semper eadem" "always the same"!

Mainly Quakers, and Puritans from Virginia first settled Talbot County in the 1650's. The county is named for Lady Grace Talbot, sister of the second Lord Baltimore and wife of Sir Robert Talbot, who were Catholics. The county became one of the most affluent in the colonies with many of the families intermarrying – the Lloyds, Tilghmans, Goldsboroughs, to name a few.

Captain John Smith sailed up the Sassafras River in 1608. It is named for the Indians who lived here and the sassafras tree's medicinal bark.

Dorchester County was originally called Dorset for Sir Edward Sackville, the 1st Earl of Dorset. The county became a political entity in 1669. Cambridge is the county seat.

Kent County was first explored by Captain John Smith in 1608. Kent County was founded in 1642 and named for Kent, England from which many of the earliest colonists had come. The first legislature convened in 1649. In 1650 James Ringgold settled on a 1200 acre land grant, called Huntingfield on Eastern Neck. He established the first settlement as New Yarmouth, but in 1706 with the founding of Chestertown, this now became the economic center and port. Crops, grain and timber as major products replaced tobacco.

The Mason-Dixon Line is a 233 mile line surveyed 1763-67 by the English surveyors Charles Mason and Jeremiah Dixon to settle a boundary dispute between the Calvert and Penn families, proprietors of Maryland and Pennsylvania respectively. Stones are placed every mile. Every fifth marker is a "crownstone" bearing the arms of the Calverts on one side and the Penns on the other. The first of these stones is on State Route 54. The Mason-Dixon Line was to play an important role in the Civil War by dividing North and South.

The area north of the Choptank River, covering Tilghman's Island, Tilghman's Neck, and the Poplar Islands, is called Bay Hundred. The name comes from the early division of Maryland into "hundreds". This is a term that dates from the Anglo-Saxon period in England, where an English "Hundred" contained ten families, ten estates of fighting men.

Pocomoke is an Indian word that means "black water". The Pocomoke River flows from Delaware through Worcester County to the Pocomoke Sound of the Chesapeake Bay. This is a swampy area and has been a refuge for soldiers, conscripts, and during the Civil War as a conduit for the Underground Railroad.

The Miles River was once named St. Michael's River, but the Quakers who disliked saintly names changed this.

Choptank means "flowing in the wrong direction". The Choptank River is the longest river on the Eastern Shore and is navigable for 53 miles. The Choptank were an Indian tribe. The General Assembly created the Choptank Reservation in 1698, but by 1800 all the Choptank tribe had disappeared.

The Frederick C. Malkus Bridge crosses the Choptank River to Cambridge. This replaced the Gov. Emerson C. Harrington Bridge, dedicated by President Roosevelt and costing $1.5 million. The bridge is now a fishing pier. The Malkus Bridge cost $37.2 million in 1987 and is named for a Maryland legislator.

Tuckahoe is a marsh plant whose roots were used by the Indians to make bread.

Maryland route 33 was once the main road between Ocean City and the ferry at Claiborne on Kent Island, and then a ferry to Annapolis. With the building of the Bay Bridge this eliminated the need for ferries.

The Tred Avon River had a number of names over the years – Tiedhaven, Trudhaven, Treaqvon, Third Haven, Tread Haven, Trade Haven and Thread Haven.

Wicomico County was created in 1867 after the citizens of Salisbury petitioned for a separate County. Salisbury became the county seat.

Worcester County was named after the Earl of Worcester and was created from Somerset County in 1742 with Snow Hill as the county seat.

Cecil County is named for Cecilius Calvert, the second Lord Baltimore. In 1662 Augustine Herman was given 1000 acres. The county was created in 1674. At that time Kent County was a part of the county.

Caroline County during the 19th c had many flour mills. The county was created in 1763 and was named for Lady Caroline Calvert, the sister of Frederick, the last Lord Baltimore and wife of Robert Eden, Maryland's last colonial governor. When first founded elections were held at the county seat. People who owned fifty or more acres or 50 pounds of personal property or sterling were permitted to vote. Denton is the county seat. The county is mainly agricultural and once had a thriving canning industry. Poultry is also important. It is the only Eastern Shore county to not have a Chesapeake Bay or Atlantic Ocean coastline.

Col. William Richardson was born in 1735 and died in 1825. He was a member of the Maryland General Assembly 1773-76. He introduced the bill forming Caroline County in 1774. He was colonel of the "Flying Camp" of the Eastern Shore in 1776 and fought at Harlem Heights. He moved the Continental Treasury from Philadelphia to Baltimore in 1777. He is buried at Gilpin's Point which is marked by a Maryland Historical Highway Marker.

Six wonderful ladies make up an artist's group known as The Traveling Brushes. They have shows off and on and one should not miss these events. The ladies are Martha Hudson, M. Joyce Zeigler, Roberta B. Seger, Mary Ekroos, Barbara Jablin, and Elizabeth R. Ruhl. They have been painting together since 1984 when one of them was offered a cottage in Tylerton on Smith Island. A.A.R.P produced a documentary on the "Traveling brushes" with Julie Harris as Narrator.

Constance Stuart Larrabee of Chestertown began her photography career during World War II, and today instead of photographing wars she has portrayed the Eastern Shore.

The loblolly pine is a tall pine found on the Eastern Shore.

British merchant houses established a factor or agent in the American colony ports, especially for the shipment of tobacco.

A number of places on the Eastern Shore were resorts around the turn of the century. Recently the Chesapeake Bay Maritime Museum, in conjunction with the Maryland Historical Society had a wonderful exhibit "Steamboat Vacations" highlighting some of these.

- Maple Hall at Claiborne - was a resort on the Miles River run by Mrs. John Cockey.
- Pasadena – in Royal Oak offered dancing, dining and other amenities
- Betterton – once had hotels such as the Rigbie, Ericsson and Idlewhile
- Wade's Point at McDaniel was also a resort
- Love Point Resort - ferries such as the *Smokey Joe* brought guests from Baltimore for dancing and other special events
- Breezy Point in Bozman was a guest house owned by Mrs. Stella Bridges
- Safety Beach, also in Bozman, was owned by Mrs. David Edmond
- Tilghman Island was called "The Sportsman's Paradise".
- Sharp's Island – was located about 4 miles south of Tilghman Island. In 1600 the island had about 600 acres. During the 1890s this was a resort. Today only a warning light remains.

Besides Perdue Farms, the Eastern Shore is also home to a number of other facilities for raising and slaughtering of chickens. These include Allen Family

Foods in Cordova and Hurlock and Tyson Foods, Inc. in Berlin. Chickens are raised throughout the Delmarva peninsula. A major problem has been their waste, which has contributed to extensive pollution of the already fragile Bay, rivers and creeks.

The Eastern Shore had 249 canneries in 1920 according to R. Lee Burton, Jr. in his book "Canneries of the Eastern Shore". By 1980 there were only 20.

The history of each city, town and village is included in the section on each place in Chapter 3.

Map of Maryland showing Cecil, Kent, Queen Anne's, Talbot, Dorchester, Wicomico, Somerset and Worcester Counties that make up the Eastern Shore

Chapter Three

Towns, Villages and Cities of the Eastern Shore

Kent Island

Kent Island is located just across the Chesapeake Bay Bridge from Annapolis and is separated from the Eastern Shore by the Kent Narrows. It is the largest island in the Chesapeake. William Claiborne of Virginia, who built a trading port, claimed the area before Lord Baltimore in 1631. The first settlement was established on the south side of the island. Claiborne built a church, fort, farms - including starting Maryland's tobacco economy, and other buildings, though none of this exists today. He brought the first white woman to Maryland, Joane Young. The island was called Kentish Island in 1638. The first court opened in 1639. Lord Baltimore also claimed the island and the first naval battle in the colonies took place here in 1635.

Matapeake Park is named for the Native Americans that were located in this region. In 1650 non-resident Indians, by law, had to give notice to the settlers about coming onto the island.

Christ Church was founded at the fort and was moved to Broad Creek in 1652. A ferry operated from Broad Creek to Annapolis. The Maryland Assembly established a postal route in 1695 and the Broad Creek settlement became a postal stop. Nearby were the first courthouse and jail on the Eastern Shore. Broad Creek became a town in 1683. Later Stevensville, Dominion and Chester took over as ports. Tobacco, wheat and corn were the major crops.

Steamers and the railroad were later to come through Kent Island, bringing many visitors, many of whom stayed at the Love Point Hotel. The hotel had Saturday night dances, an amusement park and boardwalk. Before the opening of the Bay Bridge a ferry ran from Matapeake.

Kent Narrows was noted for seafood processing and now only has three remaining establishments. The W.H. Harris Company was founded by William Holton Harris in 1947. The Holton Harris packing house was replaced by the Crab House Restaurant in 1991.

One way to explore Kent Island is to use the Cross Island Trail that goes from the Bay to Kent Narrows.

Stevensville

Stevensville is named for Samuel Stevens, the 20th governor of Maryland. The town was developed after 1850 following the sale of two farms owned by James and Charles Stevens.

Today Stevensville is a historic district with some lovely buildings, quaint shops and nearby good seafood restaurants, especially along the Narrows. The Kent Manor Inn is one of the loveliest inns on the Eastern Shore.

Attractions:

Christ Church. 117 East Main Street. The congregation was founded in 1631. The Gothic building was built c1880. The church is listed on the National Register of Historic Places. A new church has been built at 830 Romancoke Road.

Cray House. Cockey's Lane. The gambrel roofed cottage was built c1809 by John Denny, a ship carpenter and farmer, on a tract granted to Frances Stevens in 1694 and known as Steven's Adventure. The house is of "post and plank" construction. C1842 the house was enlarged by Mary Legg. The house was deeded to the Kent Island Heritage Society by the heirs of Nora Cray in 1975. Ms. Cray had bought the house at auction in 1914 and lived there with her nine children. A meat house in the back was moved to the site.

Old Stevensville Post Office. Love Point Road. 410-604-2100. The late 19th c frame building served as the post office and is now the headquarters and gift shop for the Kent Island Heritage Society. The building appears on an 1877 map.

Stevensville Train Depot. Cockey's Lane. 410-604-2100. The depot dates c1902 and was the westernmost terminus for the Queen Anne's Railroad Company System. Steamboats were used to transport passengers across the Bay. The train ran the sixty miles from Kent island to Lewes, Delaware. The structure was moved from the northern part of Stevensville to its present location in 1988.

Stevensville Bank Building. The building was constructed between 1903-97 as the The Stevensville Bank of Queen Anne's County. It is the oldest bank building on Kent Island and is listed on the National Register of Historic Places.

Methodist Protestant Church. The church was constructed towards the end of the Civil War. The church purchased the land from the Chesapeake Lodge #59 of the Order of Odd Fellows, who had bought the land in 1851 for one penny.

Broad Creek was founded in 1686 and was a stop on the postal route established by the Maryland Assembly in 1695. Later it hosted a terminus for the two ferries from Annapolis.

Broad Creek Cemetery. The cemetery was established as the site of Christ Church between 1651-84. Three additions were added to the church from 1712 to 1826. Archeological work on the site commenced in 2003.

Love Point is a village located at the northern tip of Kent Island. The Wickes family was known to have had property here as early as 1694. A ferry operated to Baltimore from here until after World War II.

Romancoke. This was once a ferry stop on the route from Claiborne to the Western Shore. Romancoke is a Native American word that can be translated as "circling waters" or "low-lying ground". The name was given to William Claiborne's plantation at the southern end of Kent Island. Mr. Claiborne was known in Virginia as Claiborne of Romancoke.

Kent Fort Manor Marker. Kent Fort Manor Road. This marks the original Claiborne settlement on the Eastern Bay in 1631.

Cross Island Trail. The 5½ mile path is perfect for biking, jogging or just a good hike.

Shopping:

Kent Island Federation of Art. 405 Main Street. 410-643-7424. The gallery sponsors art sales, exhibits and instruction.

Paul Reed Smith Guitars. 380 Log Canoe Circle. 410-643-9970. This noted guitar maker gives factory tours by reservation.

Chesapeake Chocolates. 202 Island Plaza Court. 410-643-7884. This specialty chocolate shop produces fine chocolates in the shape of crabs, Chesapeake Bay retrievers and other nautical motives.

Lodging:

Kent Manor Inn & Restaurant. 500 Kent Manor Drive. Stevensville. 410-643-5757. Entering the road down to the inn you pass towering corn fields and enter a bygone era. The inn sits on a 226 acre tract once called Smithfield, which included "The Courthouse", now "Wetherell" granted to Thomas Wetherell in 1651. The left wing was constructed in 1820 and the center section just prior to the Civil War.

Kent Manor Inn

Chester River Inn. Tackle Circle Road. 410-643-3886. Built c 1857-60 by the Tolson family on land once owned by William Body and called Body's Neck in 1650.

Dining

Kent Manor Inn. 500 Kent Manor Drive. 410-643-7716
Kentmorr Restaurant. Kentmorr Road. 410-643-2263
Hemingway's. 375 Pier One Road. 410-643-2722
Chesapeake Bay Beach Club. Rte. 8. 410-640-1933
Love Point Café. 401 Love Point Road. 410-604-5330
Verna's Island Inn. 800 Main Street. 410-643-2466
Silver Swan Restaurant. 412 Congressional Drive. 443-249-0400
Big Bats Café. 216 St. Claire Place. 410-604-1120
Tavern on the Bay. 500 Marina Club Road. 410-604-2188
Castle Marina Inn. 205 Tackle Circle. 410-604-0064
Fred's Grapevine Restaurant and Beano's Coffee & Bagels. 410 Thompson Creek Mall 410-643-4640
Hong Kong Restaurant. 148 Kent Landing. 410-643-9337
Jitterbug's Dairy Crème. 1227 Shopping Center Road. 410-643-5151
Lola's Dockside Cafe. Bay Bridge Marina. 410-643-3601

Sandwich Mill. Thompson Creek Mall. 410-643-7808
Sheridan's Irish American Grill. 410 Thompson Creek Mall. 410-643-7700
Short Stop Pizza. Thompson Creek Road. 410-643-7220

Kent Narrows

Kent Narrows separates Kent Island from the Eastern Shore. The Narrows connects the mouth of the Chester River and the Miles River. Once the area was home to commercial seafood processing with twelve operating packing houses.

Attractions:

Chesapeake Exploration Center. Piney Narrows Road. 410-604-2100. The center has exhibits on the culture and history of the area. "Our Chesapeake Legacy" is a hands-on interactive exhibit.

Lodging:

Chester Peake Waterftont B&B. 101 Swan Cove Lane. 410-757-0248

Dining:

The Narrows. 3023 Kent Narrows Way S. 410-827-8113.
Harris' Crab House. 433 Kent Narrows Way. 410-827-9500.
Anglers Restaurant & Marina. 3015 Kent Narrows Way S. 410-827-6717
Annie's Paramount Steak and Seafood House. 500 Kent Narrows Way N. 410-827-7103
Fisherman's Inn. Kent Narrows. 410-827-8807
Crab Deck. Kent Narrows. 410-827-6666
The Jetty at Margarita Grille Paradise Restaurant. 201 Wells Cove Road. 410-827-8225
The Jetty Restaurant & Tiki Bar. Rte. 50, Exit 42, Kent Narrows. 410-827-8225

Chester

Attractions:

James E. Kirwan Museum. The house was home to former Maryland State Senator James E. Kirwan. The store was built in 1889 from lumber that had floated down the Susquehanna River to the Bay after the Johnstown flood. Mary Katherine Kirwan willed the property to the Kent Island Heritage Society.

Dining:

New Canton II. Kent Town Market & Rte. 50. 410-643-6688
Pasta Prima. 2126 DiDonato Drive. 410-643-5300
Roma Restaurant. Kent Towne Market. 410-643-7579
The Canopy Restaurant. 115 S. Piney Creek Road. 410-643-9173
Heavenly Donuts Café. 2112 DiDonato Drive. 410-643-8051
Café Iguana. Rainbow Plaza. 410-604-6400
Gravity Lodge. 51 Piney Narrows Road. 410-604-6355
Meighans Pub. 205 Tackle Circle. 410-643-6554

Grasonville

Grasonville was named for William Grason (1786-1868) who was born in Queen Anne's County and was the 28th governor of Maryland.

Attractions:

Chesapeake Bay Environmental Center. 600 Discovery Lane. 410-827-6694. 500 acres of wetlands with trails, observation towers, boardwalk and exhibits.

Lodging:

Lands End Manor on the Bay. 232 Prospect Bay Drive. 410-827-6284. This gracious home was once called Prospect Plantation. For several years it was a private hunting lodge.
Holiday Inn Express. Rte. 50, Exit 42. 410-827-4454
Comfort Inn. 3101 Main Street. 800-828-3361
The Chesapeake Motel and Conference Center. 107 Hissey Road. 410-827-7272
Holly's Motel. Rte. 50 and Jackson Creek Road. 410-827-8711
Sleep Inn. 101 VFW Avenue. 410-827-5555

Dining:

Holly's. Rte. 50 and Jackson Creek Road. 410-827-8711
Chesapeake Chicken & Rockin' Ribs. Hissey Road & Rte. 50. 410-827-0030
Cove Grill. 411 Winchester Creek Rd. 410-827-7800
La Piazza Pizza & Restaurant. 4701 Main Street. 410-827-9000
Meredith Seafood & Carry-out. 3227 Main Street. 410-827-7737

Queenstown

Queenstown is located on the Chester River. The town was created in 1707 and was built on 100 acres of land of Bowingly plantation. This the first county seat of Queen Anne's County and a port during the War of 1812. In 1813 the British attacked Queenstown with 1400 men in two groups. They were forced to return to their ships when 18 men routed one group and the other group landed in the wrong place and were cut off from town by Queenstown Creek. The town shipped grain, hemp, and tobacco.

Attractions:

Colonial Court House. Rte. 18 and Del Rhodes Avenue. 410-827-7646. The c1708 one room court house was the first built in Queen Anne's County. The brick part was added c1830. The county seat was moved to Centreville in 1782. Queenstown purchased the building in 1977 which now has exhibits on the town's history.

My Lord's Gift. This 1,000 acre tract was given to Henry Coursey by Charles Calvert, third Lord Baltimore in 1658. This has now been broken up and little is known about the property.

Peace and Plenty. Rte.18. This brick two story home dates from just before the Revolution. Private home.

St. Peter's Catholic Church. Rte. 50. This church dates from the early 19th c, but the first Jesuits who came to Kent Island c 1639 founded the congregation. The present church was built between 1823-27 and the apse, nave and vestibule added in 1877. The church is listed on the National Register of Historic Places.

Bloomingdale. U.S.50. Private home. Originally called Mount Mill in 1665, this home was built in 1792 for Thomas Johnings Seth. This is a fine example of a federal home. In the 1820s Edward Harris acquired the property and renamed it Bloomingdale. The house is listed on National Register of Historic Places.

Bowingly. Private home.The property was surveyed in 1658 for James Bowling as "Bowingly" and patented to John Tully in 1660. The house was constructed in 1733 for Ernault Hawkinson on a tract that his father had purchased. From August 20-30, 1813 the British led an attack by Sir James Napier under Sir John Warren at "Bowingly". The forces failed to capture the American troops and the British retreated to Kent Island Narrows. The property was bought by the Queen Anne's Railroad Company in 1897 and turned into a hotel and amusement park.

Bennett Point Cemetery and Chapel. Recently archeologists unearthed what is probably the oldest tombstone in Maryland. It reads "Thomas Greene, Mariner at New Castle on Tyne; died at sea, 1674". A chapel with tombs was built here as early as 1698 by the Sayer family. Col. Peter Sayer was a confident of Lord Baltimore. A larger chapel was built in accordance with Richard Bennett's will in 1749. Dorothy Blake Carroll, the wife of Charles Carroll, a surgeon, and mother of Charles Carroll the Barrister, is buried here.

St. Luke's Episcopal Church. The church was constructed in 1840-41on land donated by the owners of "Bowingly" and consecrated by Bishop William Whittingham in 1842.

Pintail Point Farm. The farm located on the Wye River was built in 1936 for the Canaveros family. Today the farm specializes in sporting clays, hunting and fishing.

Wye of Carmichael United Methodist Church. The church was founded in 1873 on land donated by Judge Richard B. Carmichael. The present church was built in 1905 James and Thomas Dodd gave the logs and the lumber was sawed their mill. It was remodeled in 1948.

Lodging:

The Manor House. 511 Pintail Point Lane. 410-827-7029. English Tudor style house built in 1936 and located on the Wye River.
Queenstown Inn B&B. 7109 Main Street. 410-827-3396. The house was built c 1830s. Before 1858 Dr. Winchester, inventor of the hypodermic syringe, owned the property. In the early 1900s the bank and post office also operated here.
Irish Bed and Breakfast. 511 Pintail Point Road. 410-827-7029
Stillwater Inn B&B. 7109 Second Avenue. 410-827-9362. This home was built in 1904 for Dr. Wilmer Adams. From 1907-39 it became the Vestry of Wye Parish.

Dining:

Potter's Pantry. 714 Main Street. 410-827-8846

Shopping:

Prime Outlets is located at the junction of 50 East and 301 North.

Centreville

Situated around a town square, Centreville exemplifies some of the quaintness found in so many of the Eastern Shore towns. The Corsica River flows from here to the Chesapeake Bay. The river was originally known as Corsica Creek, but was changed to river by a legislative act in 1886.

The settlement of St. Paul's Parish dates back to 1692. Centreville replaced Queenstown as the county seat of Queen Anne's County in 1782. The town was incorporated in 1794. The town was originally named Chester Springs, but was changed to Centreville in 1797. Charles Willson Peale, the famous American painter, was born in 1741 near Centreville.

Attractions:

Queen Anne's County Courthouse. 100 Courthouse Square. 410-758-0216. This is the oldest courthouse in continuous use in Maryland and was built between 1792-94. The building was enlarged in 1876. County records date back to 1706. In front is a statue of Queen Anne (British queen 1702-14) dedicated by HRH Princess Anne and donated to the county by Arthur Houghton, founder of the Wye Institute..

Tucker House. 124 South Commerce Street. 410-604-2100. The house was built c1794. This is one of the oldest houses in Centreville and has a lovely herb garden. The house was originally two rooms deep and one room wide, and is on the second lot in Centerville to be sold. The house was enlarged c1815. The Tucker family purchased the house in 1898. The house is the museum for the Queen Anne's County Historical Society.

Queen Anne's Museum of Eastern Shore Life. 126 Dulin Clark Road. 410-604-2100. The museum has displays of the region's agricultural and maritime traditions.

St. Paul's Episcopal Church. 301 South Liberty Street. This is the third St. Paul's Church. The Communion silver dates to 1717. The church dates from c 1672, when it cost 14,395 pounds of tobacco to build. The present church was constructed in 1834, enlarged in 1855 and 1892-95. The parish hall was added in 1908-09. A biblical herb garden is located on the south lawn.

Wright's Chance. 119 South Commerce Street. 410-604-2100. This c1744 house was built on an original tract patented in 1681 and moved to its present site in 1964 on land patented to William Hemsley of Chesterfield. The Queen Anne's County Historical Society restored and owns the house. It contains items owned by William Paca of Wye Island and Annapolis, and includes Chippendale and

Hepplewhite furniture and Canton china. A smokehouse behind the house is part of the original which Mary Hopper Nicholson deeded to her daughter Henrietta, wife of Dr. Robert Goldsborough, in 1792. The garden is maintained by the Queen Anne's County Garden Club.

Wright's Chance

Kennard School. Rte. 304. The school was built in 1936 and was the first and only secondary school for blacks in Queen Anne's County. It was named for Mrs. Lucretia Kennard Daniels, who with Mr. Larrie Jones raised the money to purchase the land. The 4 room structure cost $2,600.

Chesterfield. 408 Chesterfield Avenue. Private. In 1670 Lord Baltimore granted William Helmsley a tract of 400 acres on the north side of Corsica Creek. The Court House and county jail were built on two acres given by Elizabeth Nicholson. The first house on the Chesterfield property was destroyed by an Indian attack in the 1700s. The Georgian style house was built after this and razed in 1908. The present clapboard house was recently renovated.

Gunston Hall School. 410-758-0620. This preparatory school was founded in 1911. Middleton House was the hunting lodge for Samuel and Mary Middleton, the founders of Gunston Hall. The house was constructed c1890 in the Queen Anne style.

Hope School. The school is first mentioned in the accounting records of the Board of School Commissioners in 1865 and in land records in 1892. The one room school housed grades one to seven. The school closed in 1938.

Yellow Brick House. Water Street and Banjo Lane. Judge Richard Bennett Carmichael lived in this house. He was a state circuit court judge who believed the Confederate states had the right to secede. However he believed Maryland should stay in the Union. In May 1862 Union soldiers arrested him for treason. He was released in December and resumed his duties.

202 S. Liberty Street. Private home. William Hackett left the property and house to his son Henry in 1805. The house has an unusual double staircase that leads to a single staircase.

Queen Anne's County Art Council. 206. S. Commerce Street. Centreville. 410-758-2520. The council presents art and cultural events.

Lodging:

Rose Tree B&B. 116 S. Commerce Street. 410-758-3991. The house was built in 1794, formerly the James Croney House.
Hillside Motel. 2630 Centreville Road. 410-758-2270
Comfort Suites. 160 Scheeler Road. 410-810-0555

Dining:

Julia's. 122 N. Commerce Street. 410-758-0471
Lighthouse Pub. 511 Chesterfield Avenue
Chester's Bagels & Treats. 122 N. Commerce Street
Colesseum Pizza. 112 N. Commerce Street. 410-758-1800
Hillside Steak and Crab House. 2640 Centreville Road. 410-758-1300
Corsica's Lighthouse Pub. 511 Chesterfield Avenue. 410-758-3950
Helen & Robin's County Kitchen. 105 E. Water Street. 410-758-1405
Ruthsburg Country Store & Deli. 1649 Ruthsburg Road. 410-758-2433

Church Hill

Church Hill once had six churches, but the name comes from St. Luke's Parish, which was founded in 1728.

Attractions:

St. Luke's Episcopal Church. Rte.19. This is the oldest brick church in Maryland, dating back to 1732. The church cost 140,000 pounds of tobacco. The interior of the church was destroyed during the Civil War, but restored in 1881. The parish house behind the church was built in 1817 and was used as the first public school in the county. The church is on the National Register of Historic Places.

Readbourne. Rte. 19. The original house was built in 1734 by Col. James Hollyday who married Sarah Covington Lloyd, widow of Edward Lloyd, the owner of Wye House. The original staircase and some paneling are now at the Winterthur Museum in Delaware.

Kennersley. On Chester River near Church Hill. This was formerly known as Finley Farm and is a gracious brick private home.

Church Hill Theater, Inc. 103 Walnut Street. 410-758-1331. This art deco theater was built in 1929by Elwood F. Colman and used as a town hall. In 1935 it was converted into a movie theater. Fire destroyed much of the building in 1944 and later restored. Today the theater is the community arts center for Queen Anne's County.

Dining:

Ethel's Sub Shop. Main Street. 410-556-6388

Crumpton

Crumpton on the Chester River was founded in 1759. Originally the town had been called Callister's Ferry for Henry Callister who had bought a farm on the river. Callister's Ferry, a rope raft, operated between the north and south sides of the river. The ferry continued to operate until 1865 when a bridge was built. The town is now named for William Crump on whose land the town was built. In 1858 James C. Shepperd and Maurice Walsh of Salem, NJ bought the tract and laid out the town. The movie *Showboat* by Edna Ferber was filmed near here.

The town has gone through a revitalization period. Every Wednesday an antiques auction is held at Dixon's Furniture located at Rte. 544 and 290.

Lodging:

Cole House B&B. Rte. 290. 410-928-5514. This home was built c 1840 and once served as a grocery and post office.

Chestertown

Chestertown rates as one of the most beautiful and historic towns on the Eastern Shore. Driving into town from the south across the Chester River one is left breathless by the elegant 18th and 19th century homes with gracious lawns rolling down to the river. There are a number of good restaurants and the White Swan Tavern has been an inn since 1733. There are also many antique and gift shops. Once here you may never want to leave. The best time to explore is during the week, when there are not hoards of people.

Chestertown was once called New Town. The first courthouse was built in 1697, and the town laid out in 1706 on one hundred acres divided into equal lots. On April 19, 1706 the Act for Advancement of Trade and Erecting Ports and Towns in the Province of Maryland was signed into law. New Town was made a port of entry for Cecil, Kent and Queen Anne's counties. Much of the trade was with the West Indies. Prior to 1715 the main crop was tobacco. Chestertown was also a ship auction center.

Chestertown was a port during the Revolutionary War. In 1774 a protest was held against the Tea Tax near the Customs House. Chestertown staged its own "Tea Party". The Geddes brigantine was boarded and the cargo thrown overboard. This event is still reenacted each year in May.

Chestertown received its present name in 1780 and is the seat of Kent County.. Washington College was founded here in 1782. Family fortunes were made from agricultural products such as wheat, corn and hogs and as merchants. The *Kent County News* is "A Direct Descendant of the Chestertown Spy" established in 1793 and one of the oldest newspapers in the United States. The *Chestertown Telegraph* was founded in 1825 by Nathaniel Mitchell. The steamboat *B.S. Ford* and other steamers made daily trips to Baltimore during the 19th.

Four U.S. Senators – Philip Reed, Ezekiel Foreman Chambers, James Alfred Pierce, and George Vickers lived in Chestertown. William Beck Nicholson spent 16 years in major league baseball and in 1944 hit 4 consecutive home runs.

Attractions:

Chestertown has an excellent walking tour map and booklet on the numbered historic buildings.

Geddes - Piper House. 101 Church Alley. 410-778-3499. The property was purchased in 1755 by William Geddes, King's Customs Collector for the Port of Chestertown. He sold the lot to James Moor. It was later sold to James Piper, a merchant who built the house in 1784. The Kent County Historical Society purchased the property in 1958.

135 Queen Street. This house was built in 1760 and was owned by John Bolton, who served as commissary for the Kent County Militia during the Revolutionary War.

Customs House. 103 High Street. Samuel Massey built the after purchasing the lot in 1745. He sold it in 1749 to the Ringgold family. Part of the building is presently used by Washington College's Archeology Lab.

River House. 107 N. Water Street. Built by Richard Smythe, son of Thomas Smythe of Widehall in 1784-87. The three story Federal style house was once the home of the first president of the Board of Visitors and Governors of Washington College, Peregrine Letherbury. The house is now owned by the Maryland Historic Trust. The paneling from the second floor parlor is at the Winterthur Museum and is known as the Chestertown Room.

Sterling Castle. 107 South Mill Street. The tradesman's house was built in the 18th c. The house was deeded by Charles Scott to Robert Sterling in 1756 for five shillings as a wedding present for his marriage to Anne Scott. Mr. Scott was forced to sell the house in 1759 to satisfy a debt to a shipping firm in Bristol, England. The house was bought in 1771 by Ralph Story, a shipwright. The house is a partial telescope house.

Emmanuel Protestant Episcopal Church. Cross Street. The church was erected in 1767-72 as a chapel of ease for Chester Parish, though a church had previously occupied the site since 1707. The rector Dr. William Smith presided over the convention that changed the name from Anglican Church of the United States to the Protestant Episcopal Church. Dr. Smith had come from Scotland in 1751 and was the first provost of the College of Philadelphia (Now the University of Pennsylvania). He also founded Washington College and was elected Maryland's first Episcopal bishop in 1784. This bid was later withdrawn because he had participated in the revision of the 1785 Book of Common Prayer. He returned to the College of Philadelphia. The church was renovated in the 1860s in the Victorian style. The cemetery was located on the grounds until 1860 when the courthouse was built.

Methodist Meeting House. Spring and High Streets. This house of worship was built 1801-3 and was the first permanent Methodist Church in Kent County.

Hynson-Ringgold House. Cannon and Front Streets. The house was built on land owned by Nathaniel Hynson in 1735. Dr. William Murray purchased the lot in 1743 and built the front part of the house. In 1767 Thomas Ringgold, a wealthy merchant and member of the Stamp Act Congress later purchased the house for his son who added the back wing in 1772. William Buckland may have designed the antler staircase. U.S. Senator James Alfred Pearce later bought the house. The house has an antler staircase and hip roof. Since 1944 this has been home for presidents of Washington College. The east room of the original wing was moved to the Baltimore Museum of Art in 1932.

Masonic Building. Park Row and Lawyer's Row. The Masonic Lodge was built in 1827.

Kent County Court House. Court Street. The courthouse was constructed in 1860 at a cost of $11,254. The Civil War Monument in front of the courthouse was erected in 1917.

Fountain Park. High Street. The fountain is crowned by Hebe, goddess of youth and beauty, and was erected in 1899.

Nicholson House. Queen Street. The Federal style was built in 1788 for Capt. John Nicholson who served in the Continental Navy in command of the *Horne*t and with his brother Samuel of the *Deane* during the Revolutionary War. The *Deane* took the last naval prizes of the War and was the only frigate retained by the navy after the war.

The Perkins House. 115 Water Street. This brick house was built c1740.

Frisby House. 110 Water Street. The building was completed c1770 as a townhouse for the McHard family.

Schooner Sultana (Photo courtesy of Sultana Project, Inc.)

Schooner *Sultana.* 105 S. Cross Street. 410-778-5954. The original boat was built in Boston as a cargo schooner, and then purchased by the British Royal Navy in 1768 which monitored colonial shipping mainly in the Chesapeake Bay region between 1768 and 1772. The present schooner was launched on March 24, 2001. The Schooner Sultana Project was an undertaking of the Chester River Craft and Art, a nonprofit organization, to build and operate a reproduction of the schooner *Sultana.* While the boat was being constructed students learned the crafts of traditional shipbuilding while working on an authentic model. The schooner provides hands-on educational experiences for children and adults, focusing on the culture, history and the Chesapeake Bay.

Wickes House. 102 High Street. Private home. This c1769 home once served as a tavern owned by Samuel Beck. The house has 15 fireplaces and eight bedrooms, and a walled boxwood garden.

Buck-Bacchus House and Store. High and Queen Streets. John Buck of Bideford, Devonshire, England purchased the property in 1735 as a storehouse for goods he shipped to England.

Molloy House. High Street. Mrs. Dorothy Molloy gave this 19th c house to the Maryland Historical Trust in 1971.

Widehall. 101 Water Street. Private home. The house was built c1770 in the Georgian style for Thomas Smyth, Kent County's wealthiest merchant and shipbuilder. He was a member of the local Committee of Correspondence of 1774 and head of Maryland's provisional government until 1776 when the state's first constitution was framed. He was also the first treasurer of Washington College. It was later owned by Robert Wright, governor of Maryland 1806-09 and Ezekial Chambers, U.S. Senator in the 1820's and Maryland judge.

Wide Hall

William Barroll House. 108-10 E. High Street. This house was built c1735 for William Barroll V.

Palmer or "Rock of Ages" House. 532 High Street. This home was built in the 18th c from stone that the builder, Captain Palmer, brought over as ballast from England. The house is embossed on the silver which was presented to the battleship *Maryland*. The silver is at the State Capitol in Annapolis.

109 Queen Street. This house was the Episcopal rectory from 1850 to 1910.

Washington College. The Rev. Dr. William Smith founded Washington College in 1782. The college was built 1783-88 by members of Philadelphia's Carpenters Company and patterned after Nassau Hall at Princeton. The original building was destroyed by fire in 1827 The 10th oldest institution of higher learning in the US is the only college to receive George Washington's consent to use his name. He did visit the college in 1784 and contributed $233.33 to the Endowment Fund. President Washington was given an honorary degree of doctor of laws in 1789.

Washington College

Bunting Hall. Washington College. The president of Washington College has a portrait of George Washington, painted by Rembrandt Peale in 1803 hanging in the office.

Fairlee Manor, near Centreville, was owned by actress Tallulah Bankhead who donated it to the Easter Seals Society for a summer camp.

Lyceum Theatre. High Street. The Prince Theatre was built in the 1920s by L. Bates Russell and was known as the New Lyceum Theatre or Chester Lyceum Theatre. Mr. Russell was a pioneer in the moving picture industry, owned the first car dealership in Chestertown and started *The Enterprise* newspaper.

Grand Army of the Republic building. South Queen Street. The building was constructed in 1908 as a meeting place for a black Union Veteran's organization founded in 1866. The organization acted as a charity to care for the soldiers, their widows and orphans. Ella Fitzgerald and musician Chick Webb were hosted here in 1937. in 1950 the building was sold to the Centennial Beneficial Association and renamed Centennial Hall. The only surviving G.A.R. building in the United States, it is presently being restored.

Chester River Bridge. The first bridge across the river was constructed in 1820 by the Chester River Bridge Company formed by an act of the state legislature and cost $20,000. Tolls were collected to cross the bridge. A raised draw was added in 1846.The bridge was purchased by Queen Anne and Kent Counties in 1890 and the toll eliminated. Smoking and swimming under the bridge were banned. A bridge was built in 1930 and the present one dates to 1988-89.

Bethel AME Church. Princess Street. The church contains some of its original furnishings including the altar rail, stained glass windows and pews.

Thomas Cuff House. Thomas Cuff, a free black, owned this house from 1820-1858. He owned additional property at Scott's and was a founding member of the Bethel Church. The house was restored in 1989.

Richauds Branch-Langford Road, just outside Chestertown, was one of the first turnpikes in the American colonies. Tench Tilghman, Secretary and Aide to General Washington, rode this route from Virginia to Philadelphia to inform the Continental Congress of General Cornwallis' surrender during the Revolutionary War. At Richaud's and Baker's Lane is the second site of the Hynson Chapel. All that remains today is the cemetery. Also on this road is Remington Farms, a wildlife preserve open to the public. The Remington Arms Corporation, which developed a demonstration program for raising and harvesting crops for feeding game birds, owns the farm. On the property is Broadnox, a house built 1704-08 by Robert Dunn. The house received its name from Thomas Broadnox who surveyed the land in 1658.

Stam Hall. High Street. Stam Hall houses the town clock. It was built in 1886 and was also used as a post office and theater.

Janes United Methodist Church. Cross and Cannon Streets. This Methodist church was built as an African American Church.

Cliffs School House. Quaker Neck Road. 410-778-2133. By appointment. The schoolhouse was built in 1878 and operated as a school until 1939. This was the last one room schoolhouse in Kent County. The Chester-Sassafras Foundation restored the building and in 1993 The Port of Chester Chapter of International Questers did further work.

Stepne Manor. This home was built in 1690. Mary Tilghman, widow of Dr. Richard Tilghman lived here, as did her daughter Rebecca who married Simon Wilmer. The Wilmers added a brick section to the back of the house that included a kitchen. Simon Wilmer II was deeded the house. He was responsible for laying out the county seat of Chester town and opened a gristmill on the property. In 1801 Simon Wilmer IV sold the house to Thomas Worrell. But in 1809 it was sold back to a Wilmer cousin, Joseph Nicholson Gordon, who was at the Battle of Caulk's Field. It has since changed hands many times, but the property remains intact and still includes a racetrack and stable.

Lodging:

The Imperial Hotel. 208 High Street. 410-778-5000. Lovely Victorian Hotel that also serves delicious meals.
The White Swan Tavern. 231 High Street. 410-778-2300. The inn was built before 1733 as a tannery. Joseph Nicholson bought the property in 1733. He was a member of the Committee of Correspondence and a founder of Washington College. His two sons were famous naval officers during the Revolutionary War. In 1793 John Bordley bought the house for overnight visitors to his tavern. In the 1850s it became a general store. The inn serves afternoon tea.
Great Oak Manor. 10568 Cliff Road. 410-778-5943. Lovely Georgian home on property that once numbered 1100 acres, but now has only 12 acres.
Great Oak Lodge. 410-778-2100
Parker House. Spring Avenue. 410-778-9041. The Parker house was built in 1876.
Brampton Inn. 25227 Chestertown Road. 410-778-1860. Greek revival built 1860 and listed on the National Register of Historic Places
Widow's Walk Inn. High Street. 410-778-6455. This dates to c 1877.
Lauretum Inn B&B. Rte. 20. 410-778-3236. Once owned by U.S. Senator George Vickers (1801-79). The name means "Laurel Grove" in Latin.
Claddaugh Farm B&B. 410-778-4894
The River Inn Bed and Breakfast at Rolph's Wharf. 1008 Rolph's Wharf Road. 410-778-6347. The 1830s Victorian house is located on the Chester River.
Pratt-Perry House. 224 Washington Avenue. 410-778-2734
Comfort Suites. 160 Scheeler Road. 410-810-0555
Bittersweet Suites. 410-778-2300
Hill's Inn B&B.114 Washington Avenue. 410-778-1926
Courtyard Inn. 6336 Church Hill Road. 410-778-2755
Driftwood Inn. 410-778-3200
Mattie Dean. 410-778-0255

Dining:

Imperial Hotel Hubbard Room Restaurant & Bar. 208 High Street. 410-778-5000
Andy's Pub. 337 High Street. 410-778-6779
Old Wharf Inn. Cannon Street. 410-778-3566.
Black Eyed Susan . 601 Washington Avenue. 410-778-1214
Feast of Reason. 203 High Street. 410-778-3828
La Ruota Ristorante. 323 High Street. 410-778-9989
Play it Again Sam. 108 S. Cross Street. 410-778-2688
Blue Heron Café. Cannon Street. 410-778-0188
Bluebird Tavern. 512 Washington Street. 410-778-2885
Ellen's Coffee Shop. 205 Spring Avenue. 410-810-1992
Bayside Bagels. Washington Square. 410-778-1101
C-Town Deli. 511 Washington Avenue. 410-778-3119
Luisa's Café. 14 Washington Square. 410-778-5360
China House. Kent Plaza Shopping Center. 410-778-3939
Clark's General Store. 410-778-9881
The Crystal Decanter. 337 High Street. 410-778-6849
Kettledrum Tea Room. 117 S. Cross Street. 410-810-1399
O'Connor's Pub & Restaurant. 844 High Street. 410-778-3566
Procolino's Pizzeria. 410-778-5900
Downey's Restaurant. 713 Washington Avenue. 410-778-2128
Mears Great Oak Landing Restaurant. 22170 Great Oak Landing Road. 410-778-21620
The Old Mill Bakery & Café. 207 S. Cross Street. 410-810-8841

Tolchester

In 1659 400 acres were surveyed for William Tolson. The only battle during the War of 1812 took place here in 1814. The British officer Sir Peter Parker landed forces here, but was killed in the battle known as Caulk's Battle. Tolchester was built as a fancy resort in 1877 complete with hotel, racetrack and steamers to carry people to other parts of the Chesapeake. The *Emma Giles* was one of the better known steamboats that came down from Baltimore and *Pilot Boy* from the western shore.

It's hard to believe this was once such a bustling resort. There was a roller coaster, a carousel and the Tolchester Hotel. Yes, it has lovely views across the Chesapeake and was not far from Baltimore and Annapolis. Today it is a special getaway with a nice marina and lovely old B&B.

Attractions:

Caulk's Battlefield. Caulk's Field Road
Caulk's Field House. This home was built in 1743

Lodging:

The Inn at Mitchell House. Rte. 21. 410-778-6500. The oldest part of the house dates back to 1743. This is a very pastoral setting with an herb garden behind the lovely brick house.

Dining:

Channel Restaurant. 21085 Tolchester Beach Road. 410-778-0751

Gratitude

Gratitude was once called Deep Landing. The town is named for the *Gratitude*, a steamboat from Philadelphia that called here.

Rock Hall

This town dates back to 1659 and was once known as Rock Hall Crossroads. "Rock Hall Mansion" was located at the landing west of town. The town was established in 1707. Eastern Neck Island was one of the first places to be settled on the Chesapeake. The ferry used to sail from Rock Hall to the western shore. Tench Tilghman began his ride from Rock Hall to announce the surrender of the British at Yorktown to the Continental Congress in Philadelphia.

Rock Hall is only one mile square and is surrounded by the Chesapeake Bay on the west, Grays Inn Creek to the southwest, and Swan Creek on the east. The town was incorporated in 1908.

Attractions

Watermen's Museum. Next to Haven Harbour Marina. 410-778-6697. Free admission. Models of Chesapeake boats - bugeyes, log canoes, pungys, dorys, and other watermen relics.

Waterman's Museum

Waterman's statue. Route 20

Eastern Neck National Wildlife Refuge. End of Rte. 20. The preserve has hiking trails and is excellent for bird watching.

Tolchester Beach Revisited Museum. Oyster Court. 410-778-5347.The museum has exhibits on Tolchester during its resort heyday 1877-1962.

Wickcliffe. End of Eastern Neck Island Road. Maj. Joseph Wickes settled the island in 1658 and served as chief judge of the Kent County Court Major Joseph Wickes received a land grant of 800 acres c 1658 and built "Wickcliffe" at the mouth of the Chester River. Major Wickes was a member of the Provincial Assembly, a justice of the peace, and Chief Justice of Kent County.

Wickes Memorial honors Capt. Lambert Wickes, Revolutionary War hero who lived in the house and was the grandson of Maj. Wickes. He commanded vessels from Philadelphia, Chestertown and other Eastern Shore ports, including ships owned by Willing and Morris. Robert Morris was a partner of this firm. In 1770 he was elected a member of the Captains of Ships Charitable Club in Philadelphia. Mr. Wickes was the first regularly commissioned American naval officer. In 1776-77 he raided shipping vessels in the English Channel and around Ireland on board the *Reprisal*. Lambert Wickes served as captain of the *Reprisal* which carried Benjamin Franklin to France. The *Reprisal* was lost at sea, along with Lambert Wickes during a storm off Newfoundland in 1777.

Trumpington. About five miles from Rock Hall. Land grant dates from 1658. In 1687 Thomas Smythe purchased the property for 6,000 pounds of tobacco. His daughter Sarah married Matthew Tilghman, speaker of the House of Delegates 1791. The house still remains in the Smythe family.

The Mainstay. Main Street. 410-639-9133. Rock Hall's Center for the Performing and Visual Arts

Wesley Chapel. The chapel was built by the first organized Methodists in Kent County in 1852. The congregation had been formed in 1829 in a chapel.

Lodging:

Huntingfield Manor. 4928 Eastern Neck Road. 410-639-7779. This inn is located on a farm once called "The Prevention of Inconvenience".
Inn at Osprey Point. 20786 Rock Hall Avenue. 410-639-2194. Lovely inn with good dining also.
Moonlight Bay Marina and Inn. 6002 Lawton Avenue. 410-639-2660. 1950s farmhouse
Bay Breeze Inn. 5758 Main Street. 410-639-2061
Mariners Motel. 5681 S. Hawthorne Avenue. 410-639-2291

Swan Point Inn. Rte 20 and Coleman Road. 410-639-2500
North Point Marina Hotel. 410-639-2907
Swan Haven B&B. 20950 Rock Hall Avenue. 410-639-2527
Black Duck Inn. 1 Chesapeake Avenue. 410-639-2478
Carriage House B&B. Rte. 20. 410-639-2855
Haven House Homestay. 410-639-9120
Spring Cove Manor. 12060 Spring Cove Road. 410-639-2061
Tallulah's on Main. 5750 Main Street. 410-639-2596

Dining:

Watermans' Crab House. Sharp Street Wharf. 410-639-2261.
Swan Point Inn. Rock Hall Avenue at Coleman Road. 410-639-2500
Durdings Ice Cream. 5742 Main Street. Old fashioned soda fountain
Chessie's. 21321 Rock Hall Avenue. 410-639-7727
Osprey Point. 20786 Rock Hall Avenue. 410-639-2762
P.E. Pruitt's. 20895 Bayside Avenue. 410-639-7454. Has an old buy boat, P.E. Pruitt, moored at end of the dock
Bay Wolf. Rte 20. 410-639-2000. Austrian cuisine
Old Oars Inn. 5731 Main Street. 410-639-2541
Ford's Seafood, Inc. 21459 Rock Hall Avenue. 410-639-2032
Rock Hall Snack Bar. 410-639-7427
Pasta Plus. Rte. 20. 410-639-7916
JT's Rock Hall Inn. 410-639-7625
Bay Leaf Gourmet. 410-639-2700
Chesapeake Homemade Ice Cream. 410-639-9030
Muskrat Alley Café. 410-639-2855
Brahma Bulls. 5769 Main Street. 410-639-7500

Fairlee

Attractions:

St. Paul's Episcopal Church. 7579 Sandy Bottom Road. The church was one of the thirty original Anglican churches established in 1692. St. Paul's was founded in 1693, erected by Daniel Norris. Michael Miller, who is buried on the church grounds, deeded the west side of Broadnoc Creek for the church property for 2,000 pounds of tobacco. The present building dates from 1713 and was built at a cost of 70,000 pounds of tobacco. In 1714 34 pews were installed, which could be rented or purchase for 1,000 pounds of tobacco. The church was rented in 1801 as a schoolhouse. This may be the oldest church in Maryland in continuous use. St. Paul's is one of four churches on the Eastern Shore to have a semicircular apse. The actress Tallulah Bankhead was buried here in 1968. Her sister Eugenia lived nearby.

The vestry house was constructed in 1766 on land deeded to the church by Thomas Ringgold for five shillings. The house was used as a barracks during the War of 1812.

Salem Methodist Church. Built 1853

Hanesville

Attractions:

St. James Church. The church was built 1853.

Worton

Worton is named for several towns in Oxfordshire, England. The earliest mention of it is in 1765.

Attractions:

African-American Heritage Council Museum. Worton. 410-810-1416. By appointment

I.U.Episcopal Church. Worton. 410-778-6752. The church was built c1765. The initials I.U. were found on a boundary stone near the church.

Kent Farm Museum. Turners Creek Road. The property includes the Latham House c1700 and Knock's Folly House. In addition there are antiques, agricultural machinery and other artifacts.

Lodging:

Drayton Retreat Center. 410-778-2869. Coopers Lane. This brick house sits on an original grant of 1,200 acres. It has now been given to the United Methodist Church as a Retreat Center.

Dining:

Harbor House. Worton Creek Marina. 410-778-0669
Five Star Dinette. Catts Corner. 410-778-2729

Betterton

Betterton, like Tolchester, was once a resort town, and is located on "Fish Hall Farm". The town was originally known as "Crew's Landing" and was a fishing village. Steamboats brought guests to this town developed by Richard Turner. The town is named for his wife, Elizabeth Betterton. Among the famous hotels that operated here was the Rigbie built in 1902.

The town still has a beach and attracts those wishing to relax along the Chesapeake Bay. The town has been nicknamed "The Jewel of the Chesapeake". It was incorporated in 1906. The Betterton Day Celebration is held the first Saturday in August. The bridge spanning Bayside Boulevard where many young received their first kiss has recently been renovated.

Lodging:

Lantern Inn. 115 Ericsson Avenue. 410-348-5809. The inn is a restored hotel dating from 1904.

Dining:

Dublin Dock. 12 Ericsson Avenue. 410-348-5896

Kennedyville

John Kennedy of Pennsylvania bought 310 acres known as "The Tavern Farm" or "Middle Farm" here beginning in 1853. His brother William bought the 469 acre "Redgrave Farm" or "Kent Manor" and an additional 100 acres at the same time. The Kent County Railroad bought rights-of-way to lay track in the town along which building lots were platted in the 1860s. In 1865 the Baltimore & Delaware Bay Railroad came through and the Philadelphia, Wilmington & Baltimore Railroad in 1872. Agricultural products were shipped to Philadelphia and elsewhere. The railroads ceased to exist in the 20th c and eventually Kennedyville went back to being a rural community. An Amish community was established in 1954 near Kennedyville at Rte. 213 and Rte. 297.

Attractions:

Thomas Perkins House. Rte. 292. Thomas Perkins built this house in 1720. His son, Col. Isaac Perkins was a commissioner of the Maryland Council of Safety during the Revolutionary War. This group supplied George Washington's army, and much of the flour came from Col. Perkins farm. He was known as the "Flaming Patriot" during the war.

Kent Museum. Turner Creek Road. 410-348-239. The museum has agricultural artifacts, nature trails, and includes Charlie's House, Latham House c1700 and Knock's Folly house.

Grace Apostolic Congregation. Rte. 213. The church was formerly known as Grace Episcopal Church and was built by John Kennedy.

Sassafras Natural Resource Management Area. Turner Creek Road. The area has trails, places to picnic and high cliffs along the Sassafras River. It was originally named Bloomfield Farm, part of the Lincoln Land and Cattle Company.

Kent schoolhouse. Creamery Street. Private home. The school was built in 1875 and remained as a school until 1914.

United Methodist Church. The church was built in 1860 on land once owned by john Kennedy. It was formerly known as Waters Chapel.

Dining:

The Kennedyville Inn. 21 Augustine Highway. 410-348-2400
Stoltzfus Restaurant. 410-778-5300

Shrewsbury Neck

The earliest land patent for what is now Shrewsbury Neck was granted in 1659 to Richard Turner, for whom Turner's Creek is named. The area was settled in 1681, and the first frame church probably built about that time. A larger, brick church was completed in 1729. This was demolished in 1835 after the present structure was completed. Several of the rectors of the church had careers outside their ministry. Rev. James Jones Wilmer, a rector in the 1780s served as secretary of the first convention of Anglican ministers after the Revolution. This convention was held at Emmanuel Church in Chestertown. Rev. Wilmer proposed naming the Anglican Church in America the Protestant Episcopal Church.

Another patent was granted to Edward Blay in 1675 for two hundred acres at the head of Turner's Creek. He built a wharf and operated a mill on the creek. He also served as a judge on the provincial court and in 1700 negotiated a treaty with the Indians in the area. Mr. Blay was a colonel in the Cecil County Militia and a member of the Maryland Legislature 1706-07 and Kent County in 1713. He was appointed one of eight county commissioners to supervise the drawing of the boundary lines with Cecil and Kent Counties. Some of the Blay property was given to Shrewsbury Parish, and members of the family are buried there.

Buried in the graveyard is General John Cadwalader who was born in Philadelphia in 1742. In 1768 he married Elizabeth Lloyd, daughter of Col. Edward Lloyd of Wye House. Her dowry included 10,000 pounds of money, 2,478 acres of land on the Sassafras River called Shrewsbury Farm, 78 slaves, 125 horses other animals, and 427 pounds of Lloyd family plate. Gen. Cadwalader went on to become one of Philadelphia's wealthiest men. He organized the militia on the Eastern Shore in 1777 at the request of George Washington. He died at Shrewsbury Farm in 1786. His epitaph was written by

Thomas Paine.

The name may have come from the Earl of Shrewsbury, Rt. Hon. Charles Talbot, Principal Secretary of State in England under King William and Queen Mary.

Shrewsbury Parish Church. Rte. 213. This parish was established in 1692 on the Sassafras River and is the mother parish for all Episcopal Churches in Kent County, except Old St. Paul's. The present Church was completed in 1832. Frank George Wisner III, a former U.S. Ambassador, gave the copper cross as a gift to the church to Egypt. The communion service dates back to the 1700s

Shrewsbury Parish Church

Gen. John Cadwalader historical marker. Rte. 213. The marker indicates the birthplace of John Cadwalader, a friend of George Washington's and Revolutionary War general. While Washington was in office General Thomas Conway issued the "Conway Cabel" to depose Washington. Gen. Cadwalader challenged Gen. Conway to a duel and wounded him in the mouth.

Dining:

Vonnie's Restaurant. Rte. 213. 410-778-5300

Still Pond

Still Pond was originally named Steele's Pone, "Steels Favorite", from Elizabethan English. Earliest records of the town date to 1661. In 1841 Tom Hyer who lived here won the first American heavyweight boxing championship, beating Yankee Sullivan for a purse of $10,000. This was the first place to grant women's suffrage in Maryland in 1908.

Attractions:

Still Pond Methodist Church. Built 1853

Coleman

Coleman is located near Stillpond. The town is named for the Rev. John Coleman, who is thought to have lived near here, fought in the Revolutionary War and was an Episcopal minister.

Galena

Galena was founded in 1763 and incorporated in 1860. Galena was formerly named Georgetown Crossroads. The town was the site of Downs Cross Roads Tavern that served the stage route between Annapolis and Philadelphia. The town was renamed for the silver found here in 1813 and carried to Philadelphia. The mine was closed down during the War of 1812 so the British wouldn't capture it. Galena suffered devastating fires in 1893 when the entire business section burned and in 1956 when 6,000 gallons of high-octane gasoline exploded at the Kent Oil Company.

Lodging:

Rose Hill B&B. 13842 Gregg Neck Road. 410-648-5334. Rosehill Farm is one of the largest miniature rose nurseries in the U.S.
Carrousel Horse B&B. 145 Main Street. 410-648-5476.

Dining;

Dixie-Jo's. Rte. 213 & Cross Street. 410-648-5521
Village Bakery & Café. 119 N. Main Street. 410-648-6400

Georgetown

Georgetown is located on the Sassafras River, and was a Port-of-Entry, a ferry landing, and a base for Continental supplies during the Revolutionary War. The town was laid out in 1736. The British burned the town in May 1813. Georgetown was named for Frederick, brother of King George III. The Kitty Knight House is located right on the Sassafras River and is a favorite place for a meal or overnight.

Attractions:

Olivet Methodist Church. The church was built in 1842 and in 1887 renovated as a Gothic style church.

Lodging:

Kitty Knight House. Route 213. 800-404-7812. This is the only house in Georgetown and Fredericktown not burned by the British under Adm. Cockburn during War of 1812 when the owner refused to leave an elderly neighbor, and the British saved both homes.
Skipjack Cove Yachting Resort. 150 Skipjack Road. 410-275-2122.

Skipjack Cove

Dining:

The Granary. MD Route 213, on Sassafras River. 410-275-1603.
Kitty Knight House. Rte. 213. 800-404-8712
Twinney's. 410-648-5784
The Sassafras Grill. 410-275-1603

Cecilton

In 1730 a session of the General Assembly laid out land and erected a town at the junction of Scotchman's Creek (Omealy Creek) and the Bohemia River. This was to become Cecilton or what was formerly called Broxen's Point.

St. Steven's Episcopal Church. Rte. 282. The Sassafras Parish was established in 1692. The bell was presented by Queen Anne.

St. Francis Xavier Roman Catholic Church (Old Bohemia Mission). Bohemia Church Road, northeast of Cecilton. Charles Carroll, a Signer of the Declaration of Independence and his brother John, the first Catholic Bishop in the United States and founder of Georgetown University, attended the Old Bohemia Mission, which was established in 1704 by the rev. Thomas Mansell of the Society of Jesus. The property once included 1200 acres of land, a plantation house and academic Academy. The Jesuit Academy was the predecessor of Georgetown University. On the property are a farm museum, the church and rectory. Kitty Knight is buried in the cemetery.

Greenfield. Rte. 213. This private Georgian manor house was built in the 1700s on land patented to John and Mary Ward in 1674. The Ward burying ground contains Lusbys and Pascaults, who were later owners.

Lodging:

The Anchorage. Rte. 213. 410-275-1972. The Lusby family built this lovely old brick house in the early 1700s. Ruth Lusby and Commodore Jacob Jones were married in 1721 and made this their home. Comm. Jones served on the *Philadelphia* when it ran aground at Tripoli and commanded the sloop *Wasp* during the War of 1812.

The Anchorage

Earleville

Attractions:

Mount Harmon Plantation. Grove Neck Road. 410-275-8819. This Georgian manor house was built in 1730 on a 350 acre grant issued in 1651 by the Second Lord Baltimore to Godfrey Harmon. The plantation's main product was tobacco. It is now owned and operated by the Natural Lands Trust.

Cayots Corner

Cayots Corner was part of land grant where the Labadist, a Dutch Protestant Communal Sect, resided from 1660-1725. They led a communal life and disbanded c1698.

Woodstock Farm. Cayots Corner Road. Private home. The farm was once part of the Labadie tract of 3,750 acres and was owned by Dr. Petrus Bouchelle. It was obtained in 1684 from Augustine Herman. The original house burned in 1872.

The present house was built in the 1880s. The farm was home to “Kelso”, voted Horse of the Year for five consecutive years (1960-64).

Bohemia Manor. Rte. 213. This was the original manor of Augustine Herman (See Chesapeake City).

Great House Farm. Mitton Road. Private home. The farm is on the site of the Labadist Sect. Samuel Bayard inherited the property from his father Petrus Bayard who had been given the property by Augustine Herman. The Great house was constructed 1680-1721. the house faces the Bohemia River. One of the rooms is named for Rev. George Whitfield, a prominent Methodist preacher. On the grounds is a family cemetery.

Tybridge Estate. Winbak Farm. Buckworth Road. Private home. The farm is home to the yearling division of Winbak Farm, one of the largest breeders of standardbred horses in North America.

Chesapeake City

Schaefer’s Restaurant and Bridge, Chesapeake City

Chesapeake City is one of the most charming towns that has really preserved a number of downtown buildings and retained its quaintness. The city is located on the C&D Canal that connects the Delaware River and the Chesapeake Bay at the most northern end of the Eastern Shore. Augustine Herman who received a large land grant for much of the area around here envisioned building a canal as early as the 17th c. The canal was officially opened on July 4, 1829 and cost $2.25 million. The canal is fourteen miles long. The canal was purchased by the U.S. government in 1919 and has been widened and improved several times. The town was once known as "The Village of Bohemia", but changed the name to Chesapeake City in 1839.

During World War II the Bainbridge Naval Training Center, a 1,200-acre facility, trained almost five hundred thousand sailors. The center closed in 1948, but was reopened during the Korean War. When it closed for good in July 1976 it became a nuclear power school.

Attractions:

Chesapeake City has some lovely shops, antique shops, inns and restaurants along the canal. A good walking map of the city is available. Walking along the canal one can see large and small yachts, and huge ships that travel the globe. The current through the canal is very strong, and smaller boats are often swept sideways toward the bridge that crosses the canal using Rte. 213. the historic area is listed on the National Historic Registry and Maryland's Historic Registry.

Chesapeake & Delaware Canal Museum. 410-885-5621. This building was the old lock pump-house for the canal. It has a large waterwheel built in 1837 on display. The wheel used buckets to change the level of water in the locks.

The Pell Gardens provide a lovely view of the Canal.

Captain Layman House. Bohemia Avenue. Built c 1830 for the proprietor of the Bayard House.

Riley House. Bohemia Avenue. The c1831 house was a shoemaker shop and is now an art gallery.

The Cropper House. Bohemia Avenue. The original house was one room c1833. It was later enlarged and used as a general store, tinsmith's shop, post office and pool hall. Captain Cropper and his family helped found Chesapeake City.

Franklin Hall. Bohemia Avenue. This was built c 1870 and used for a hardware and harness shop.

J.M. Reed Back Creek General Store. Bohemia Avenue. The building dates c1861 and sold dry goods and merchandise from Baltimore and Philadelphia. The store is still being used.

Brady-Rees House. Bohemia Avenue. The c1870 Victorian home was owned by Henry Brady who ran the tow on the canal.

Polk House. Bohemia Avenue. Henry Brady owned this house until he moved to the Brady-Rees House. John Banks, the founder of Chesapeake City's first bank, purchased the house in 1896.

Hager-Kinter House. Bohemia Avenue. The c1915 house is a Sears & Roebuck stick house.

Town Hall. Bohemia Avenue. The c1903 building was once the National Bank of Chesapeake City. The granite came from Port Deposit.

Trinity Methodist Church. Bohmeia Avenue. The granite church was built in 1889.

The William Lindsey House. The house was built in c1854 for William Lindsey, the owner of a sawmill. Later Jack Hunter who wrote the novel, "The Blue Max", purchased the property.

Dr. Davis House. George Street. Dr. Joseph Hedrick purchased the house in 1874. He was an executive of the canal and used funds from the canal on the house. This problem was discovered and he fled to Europe with the money.

The Beiswanger Shop. George Street. The c1896 house was once a bakeshop and an ice cream parlor.

Hersh Mini Museum. 410-885-5889. By appointment. The museum holds 19th c household items and a collection of irons.

St. Rose of Lima Catholic Church. North Chesapeake City. The church was built c1874.

Lodging:

Inn at the Canal. 104 Bohemia Avenue. 410-885-5995. This building dates c 1870.
The Blue Max Inn. 300 Bohemia Avenue. 410-885-2781
Shipwatch Inn. 401 First Street. 410-885-5300
Old Wharf Cottage. Bohemia Avenue and canal. 410-885-5040

Schaefer's Canal House Cottages. 208 Bank Street. 410-885-2200

Dining:

Chesapeake Inn Marina and Restaurant. C&D Canal. 410-885-2040. good food and great views over the Canal.
Schaefer's Canal House. 208 Bank Street. 410-885-2200. The restaurant opened as a general store in 1908, and overlooks the C&D Canal and the historic district. In mid 1999 the restaurant was for sale, and it can only be hoped the name will remain the same.
Canal Creamery. 9 Bohemia Avenue. 410-885-3314. Ice cream parlor
The Tap Room Seafood Restaurant. Corner of 2nd and Bohemia. 410-885-2344.
Bohemia Café & Bakery. 2nd & George Street. 410-885-3066
Jack & Helen's Restaurant. Rte. 213. 410-885-5477
Yacht Club Restaurant. 225 Bohemia Avenue. 410-885-2267
Bakers Restaurant. 1075 Augustine Herman Highway. 410-398-2435

Bayard House. 11 Bohemia Avenue. 410-885-5040. Bayard House has won first place in the vegetable crab soup category at the Maryland Seafood Festival. It also serves a delicious crab and oyster dish with hollandaise. The building dates c 1835 and in 1911 became a hotel and bar. The inn is located on the Canal.

Bayard House

Massey

Massey was named for the Hugh Massey family who had large land holdings in this area. "Massey's Venture", a land grant consisted of 20,000 acres in Kent County. In 1877 Dr. Charles Henry Bedford Massey (1828-1891) owned 2500 acres in Massey alone. The Kent and Queen Anne's Railroad once passed through here beginning in 1868, carrying passengers and agricultural products. A cannery operated here until World War II. In 1888 a fire destroyed much of the town.

Attractions:

Massey Air Museum and Aerodrome. Rte. 330. The museum has a collection of antique airplanes and memorabilia. Flying clubs use the grass strip.

Millington

The town dates back to 1696. The earliest known business was Daniel Jacob's ferry service on the Chester River. Millington was built on a tract of land believed to have been called "London Bridge', owned by Daniel Toas (died 1691). Sarah Toas and her husband Peter Massey acquired the 350 acres, which was later sold to Gilbert Falconer who built the first bridge over the Chester River in 1724. It was originally called "Bridgetown" and later "Head-of-Chester". Thomas Gilpin, a Quaker bought the property in 1764 and ran a mill. He was a member of the American Philosophical Society which was involved in founding a shortcut between the Bay to Philadelphia. Eventually the C&D Canal would be built in Cecil County. He also invented a type of wheat that could resist mildew so it could be easily stored and shipped. Millington at this time was called Gilpinton.

The town received its present name from Richard Millington, a farmer in 1829. The town is located in both Queen Anne's and Kent Counties. Millington was incorporated in 1890. The Queen Anne's and Kent Railroad was constructed through the town in the 1860s. Large amounts of peaches were shipped from Millington. In addition to other mills in town, a woolen mill was established by English immigrants, Thomas and John Mallalieu. At one point they were producing 90,000 yards of cloth, most of which was shipped back to England. A fire devastated much of downtown in 1890.

The town once had its own baseball team. Hanson Horsey, a Millington resident, left in 1911 to become a pitcher for the Cincinnati Reds. George Wallace was a noted umpire.

Attractions:

Old Mill. Sassafras Street. The mill was built in 1766.

Dr. John Thomas House. Cypress Street. The house was built c1787 by Dr. Thomas, a physician and surgeon.

Asbury M.E. Church. Cypress Street. The first church was built in 1838 and the present church in 1872.

Millington Academy. Private home. Thomas Gilpin the younger donated the property for a school in 1813. The school burned in 1893, but was rebuilt. A new school was built in 1915 on Cypress Street.

Dining:

Deb's Place. 410-438-3177
Dutch Family Restaurant. 410-778-0507
Millington Plaza. 410-928-3239
Tailgate Market. 410-928-3136
Up the River Café. 410-928-5411

Sudlersville

Sudlersville dates from the mid 18th c and was named after the Sudler family who settled at "Sledmore". Sudler's Cross Roads became a post office in 1811, and the name was changed to Sudlersville. Famous baseball player Jimmy Foxx was born and raised here and first played baseball in Easton. He was the first baseball player to win 2 MVP awards in 1932-33, and then went on to win a third five years later. He was the youngest player to be elected to the Baseball Hall of Fame (1951). Elsie Sudler was the first female to receive a driver's license in Maryland #243 in 1910. Dr. Haydon Metcalfe, a local physician, was the first doctor on the East Coast to diagnose Rocky Mountain Spotted Fever.

Attractions:

Sudlersville Train Station Museum. 101 Linden Street. 410-604-1200. The museum dates to c 1885 and preserves the history of the railroad and Jimmy Foxx.

Dudley's Chapel. Benton Corner Road. 410-60-42100. This is the oldest Methodist church in Queen Anne's County dating to c 1783 and fifth oldest in the U.S. Bishops Cooke and Ashbury preached here. The church is unusual in that it is made of brick, while most Methodist Churches are of wood.

St. Andrew's Episcopal Chapel. S. Church and Maple Avenue. The chapel was built in 1879 and dedicated in 1880. The first St. Andrew's Chapel was built in 1730.

"Sledmore". Off Rte. 300. Dr. Arthur E. Sudler resided in this home built in 1713.

Jimmy Foxx Memorial Statue. The Sudlersville Community Betterment Club erected the lifesize bronze statue in 1997.

Hunting Lodge:

J&P Hunting Lodge. 1105 Benton Corner Road. 410-438-3832

Templeville

Templeville is on the Queen Anne's and Caroline County border. The town was originally called Bullockville or Bullock-town. In 1847 it was named after the Temple family. William E. Temple served as sheriff of Queen Anne's County in 1869. The Underground Railroad was important here are there were many free blacks.

Marydel

Marydel sits on the Maryland-Delaware border. The town was founded in 1850 and named Halltown after William Hall. It rose to national prominence in 1877 when James Gordon Bennett, the owner of the New York Herald and Frederick May, an explorer, fought an illegal duel here, after Mr. May broke his engagement to Mr. Bennett's sister, and they had had an argument. Neither man was hurt, but Mr. Bennett later moved to Paris.

Attractions:

Mason-Dixon Line Marker. The line was surveyed in 1762 by Mason and Dixon to settle the claims of the Calverts of Maryland and the Penns of Pennsylvania. The county border was placed in 1765 with 34 stones at one mile intervals.

Henderson

Native Americans inhabited Henderson for hundreds of years before Edward Thawley settled on a farm in the 18th c. The first homes were built in 1866. The town was named for a director of the Delaware and Chesapeake Railroad which ran through the town. Mud Mill operated for almost a hundred years.

Bridgetown

Lodging:

Schrader's Bridgetown Lodge. 410-758-1824. B&B located on 70 acres.

Goldsboro

The four Indian paths on the Delmarva peninsula converged in Goldsboro. Goldsboro was originally a crossroads named Oldtown. Beaver pelts were exchanged at the trading post. The name was changed in 1870 and named for Dr. G.W. Goldsborough who owned most of the land and was a state legislator. He was imprisoned at fort McHenry during the Civil War as he supported the South. In 1867 with the arrival of the railroad, the town became a canning center, mainly for tomatoes.

Castle Hall. Rte.311. This private home is a brick "telescope" house. In 1748 Robert Hardcastle acquired the property. His son, Thomas, a county justice, built the house in 1781.

Greensboro

This town, near the headwaters of the Choptank River, was founded in 1732. It was named Bridge-town. The town was resurveyed in 1791 and renamed Greensboro. Sessions of Caroline County Court were held here in 1778-80. The first bridge across the Choptank River was built here before 1732. Grain was bought by boat up the Choptank River and shipped by wagon to Frederica on the Delaware Bay and then by boat to Philadelphia. The town is named for Gen. Nathaniel Greene who had been the commander of troops from here during the Revolutionary War. Shipbuilding became an important industry.

Attractions:

K. Goldsborough House. Railroad Avenue. Judge Laird Goldsborough lived in the house from 1897-1970. He was an adjutant general in the Philippines and wrote the country's first constitution.

Peter Harrington Marker. North Main Street. 2nd Lt. Harrington served in 1778 in the 28th battalion of the Militia Caroline County. He laid out a tract of land known as Ingram's Desire and built a home. He died in 1814 is buried here on land he donated for the Methodist Meeting house in 1789.

Shopping:

Greensborough Trading Company. 105 S. Main Street. 410-482-2200. The shop showcases artisans from the Eastern Shore.

Lodging

Riverside Hotel. 204 N. Main Street. 410-482-7100. The hotel was built by Clinton Jarman, a merchant, in 1912 and cost $10,000. The hotel was reopened in 2000 after major renovations. It is located on the Choptank River.

Dining:

Greensboro Restaurant. Main Street. 410-482-8633
Harry's. 116 W. Sunset Avenue. 410-482-6758
Riverside Hotel. 204 N. Main Street. 410-482-7100
Greensboro Deli. Whiteleysburg Road. 410-482-6077
Mr. D's. 610 Sunset Avenue. 410-482-9020

Ridgely

Ridgely was laid out in 1867 by the Maryland Baltimore Land Association and Rev. Greenbury W. Ridgely, who owned several thousand acres of land. The railroad which was to transport peaches and grain provided too much competition for these products and the town suffered. From 1895-1919 canning brought prosperity. Hanover Foods survived for over 100 years.

Attractions:

Adkins Arboretum. 12610 Eveland Road. 410-634-2847. The arboretum is located on 400 acres in Tuckahoe State Park. Forested wetlands, mature forests and gardens attract hikers and nature lovers. The arboretum hosts workshops, art exhibits, lectures, garden tours, and many other events.

St. Gertrude's Monastary. 14259 Benedictine Lane. 410-634-2497. St. Gertrude's was established in 1887. An academy for girls was opened and was the only Catholic school for many years in this area. In 1959 the acdemy became the Benedictine School for Exceptional Children. Benedictine sisters live on a 500 acre farm. They are involved in education and other outreach programs, including a program for homeless/abused women and their children.

Oaklawn. Rte. 312. This private home was owned by Rev. Ridgely. He had been a law partner of Henry Clay in Lexington, KY and then became a clergyman.

Lodging:

Dunning Studio and B&B. 24451 Burnt Mill Road. 410-634-2491
Slo Horse Inn B&B. 11649 Holly Road. 410-634-2128

Dining:

Sam's Restaurant and Pizza. 7 Central Avenue. 410-634-1158
Dave's Place. 207 E. Sixth Street. 410-634-2277

Denton

Denton is located on the Choptank River, and is the county seat of Caroline County. The Maryland Assembly called for the establishment of a new county seat at Pig Point, but the Revolutionary War postponed the building of a new courthouse. Goldsboro competed for the seat. A referendum was held in 1790 when Denton, situated near Pig Point won. The land was owned by Edward Lloyd IV of Talbot County. The court house green was purchased for 120 shillings in 1791.

The town was originally named Edenton in honor of Sir Robert Eden, the proprietary governor of Maryland from 1769-1774. The "E" was dropped after the Revolutionary War. Ships came up the Choptank River from Cambridge. The area became known for its dairy products and produce. The town had a slave market on the public square. It was also an important banking center like Easton and had three commercial banks prior to the Civil War. A fireworks display heralding the end of the Civil War in 1865 caused a fire which destroyed many old buildings. Before World War I the town had a (horse) race track. Former Gov. Harry Hughes was born in Easton, but grew up in Denton.

Attractions:

Choptank River Heritage Center

Choptank River Heritage Center/Denton Steamboat Wharf Terminal. 10219 River Landing Road. 410-479-4950. The Denton Wharf was originally built in 1883 and has gone through extensive renovation. The terminal building contains a passenger waiting room, the steamship agent's office and warehouse space. The *Cambridge Lady* and other vessels now visit the terminal.

The Museum of Rural Life. 16 N. 2nd Street. 410-479-2055. The museum contains several historic buildings - "Chance's Desire" c1790, "Painter's Range" c1840, "Taylor-Brown House", c1819 and "Skillington's Right" c1795.

Museum of Rural Life

The Schoolhouse. 104 S. 2nd Street. The building served as a schoolhouse from 1883-1925. In 1926 the Denton Community Club purchased it. The Women's Club of Denton founded in 1915 as a literary society now maintains the building.

Caroline County Courthouse. Market Street. The first court house was built on this site in 1797. The building was renovated in 1895 and added on to in 1966. The courthouse is a replica of Independence Hall in Philadelphia.

Neck Meeting House. Rte. 404. The Tuckahoe Neck Meeting house was built in 1802 by members of the Society of Friends who had formerly been Nicholites, a sect in Caroline County. The building was used until 1897 and then rented out. The Choptank electric Coop-erative bought the building in 1949.

Clover Cultural Center. Main Street. 410-479-3200. This non-profit organization offers a venue for artists, writers, actors and musicians and children to encourage their creative talents.

Sophie Kerr House. Fifth Street. Sophie Kerr (1880-1965) is the author of 23 novels, many short stories, and for whom the Sophie Kerr Prize is given at Washington College. Ms. Kerr began writing novels in 1916 and in 1926 moved to New York City where she entertained on a grand scale. She received an honorary degree from Washington College in 1942 along with Eleanor Roosevelt. At the time of her death she left $573,000 to the college for the Sophie Kerr Prize, and also for scholarships, publications and purchase of books.

Her father bought 90 acres on the Choptank River in 1872. He was a noted horticulturalist, a director of a local bank, involved in civic affairs, and helped establish the first municipal cemetery.

Lodging:

Memory Lane B&B. 24700 Williston Road. 410-479-2107. The house is an Italiannate Victorian built in 1850.
Best Western Denton Inn. Rte. 313. 410-479-8400
Gilpin Point. Gilpin Point. 410-673-7625

Dining:

Market Street Café. 200 Market Street. 410-479-3100
Snappy's Bar & Grill. Denton Plaza. 410-479-5660
Colesseum Pizza. 14 Denton Plaza. 410-479-4600
Joe's Hoagie House. 601 N. Sixth Street. 410-479-3384
Bullock's Deli. 422 N. Sixth Street. 410-479-0270
China House. 16 Denton Plaza. 410-479-5600

Shopping:

Bethlehem Country Traders. Off Dover Bridge Road. Each December the store sells a limited edition of Christmas ornaments.

Andersontown

Dining:

Cohee's Restaurant & Lounge. Rte 404. 410-479-9833

Williston

Williston was also known as Potters Landing, named for Zabdiel Potter, a sea captain from Rhode Island. He built the Potter Mansion. Col. Arthur John Willis, who had a fleet of sailing packets, and for whom the town is named, bought this house in 1849. He served on the Union side during the Civil War. Williston Lake was created in 1778 by a mill dam that Gen. William Potter enlarged.

Attractions:

Williston Mill Historic District. 24729 Williston Road. A mill and miller's house are located on a mill stream. The house was built c1840-50 and enlarged c1870 and 1895. The mill was built c1830-40 and added onto in 1895. It is one of two mills remaining in Caroline County.

Hillsboro

A chapel was known to have been here as early as 1694. The English colonists used the St. Jones Indian path for trade between the Tuckahoe River and Dover, Delaware. Hillsborough was a tobacco trading town. In 1797 Hillsboro Academy was founded. Steamboats came up to four miles south of here, and freight was carried the rest of the way up the creek. A fire destroyed much of downtown in 1896.

Attractions:

St. Paul's Episcopal Church. The church was established in 1748 at Tuckahoe

Bridge. A church was built on the site in 1768. The present structure dates to 1853 and was consecrated in 1858.

Queen Anne

Queen Anne is named for Queen Anne of England, Scotland and Ireland, and the last ruler of the house of Stuart. A post office is known to have been here in 1796.

Birthplace of Frederick Douglass. Off Rte. 303. Frederick Douglass, the famous abolitionist spent the first six years of his life here with his grandmother, Betsey Bailey.
Knotts Farm. Near Queen Anne. This late 19th c home is an Italianate farm house.

Richland. Tuckahoe Creek. This house was built c1740

Tuckahoe State Park. Off Rte. 404

Cordova

Cordova was on Martenet's map in 1866 and later was located on the Pennsylvania railroad line, now the Chesapeake Railroad.

St. Joseph's Roman Catholic Church. The original part of the church was built in 1782 with additions added in 1843 and 1903.

Skipton

Skipton is first mentioned in 1662 when a court was held at the house of William Coursey of Skipton. The courthouse was built on a 20 acre site near Skipton Creek and was also an inn. The town was named York. In 1706 legislation created Queen Anne's County and the county seat was moved near Pitt's Bridge in 1710.

Skipton has several lovely homes built about 1800. Buckingham c1820 has much of its original woodwork. Skipton Farm c1800 and Skipton Landing c1820 are all private homes.

Wye Island

Wye Island is located between the Wye and Wye East Rivers near Queenstown. Much of Wye Island consists of a 2450 acre registered wildlife preserve. The island has been owned by a number of prominent Marylanders that include the Lloyd, Chew, Paca, Bordley, Stewart, Bryan, Chaire and Hardy families. The first member of the Lloyd family received a patent to the island "Lloyd's Insula" in 1688.

John Beale Bordley, a lawyer and jurist, owned half of the island south of Dividing Creek. During the 1770s he gave up his professional life to farm the land. Unlike most Maryland farmers who planted tobacco, he chose to grow wheat, vineyards, and orchards. On his plantation he manufactured textiles, had a brickyard, brewery, and processed salt from the Wye River waters.

Later this property was sold off as thirteen separate farms. Glenn and Jacqueline Stewart were to eventually purchase eight of these and turned it into a cattle ranch. They built a hunting lodge on Grannery Creek. This property was eventually sold to the Hardy brothers.

During the 1970s the Rouse Company planned to develop the land, but met with great opposition. The State of Maryland purchased the property and established the Wye Island Natural Resource Management Area.

Attractions:

Wye Plantation was once owned by Governor William Paca, a Signer of the Declaration of Independence and Governor of Maryland, as a summer home. William Paca owned half of Wye Island and built Wye Hall in the 1790s. The house burned in 1879. Henrietta Maria Lloyd married Samuel Chew. Their daughters married William Paca and John Bordley Beale. Wye Plantation was inherited by Julianna Tilghman Paca, wife of John Philemon Paca, son of William Paca. The grounds have trees over two hundred years old and elegant boxwood gardens. It is truly one of the grand Eastern Shore estates. William Paca is buried here.

Wye House. Bruff's Island Road. This house has been in the Lloyd family since 1658 when Edward Lloyd received a grant of a thousand acres. The first Wye House was built by the fourth Edward Lloyd and burned by the British. The present house was built c 1784 and has lovely gardens. The place was named after the Wye River in Wales, from where the Lloyd's had emigrated.

Stagwell was patented to Thomas Stagwell in 1649 and acquired by Richard Bennett, one of the largest landowners in Maryland, in 1706. His descendant Judge Richard Bennett Carmichael built the house c1805. He presided over the convention for a new constitution for Maryland in 1867. (Today a number of new homes are going up on this property).

Cheston on Wye was surveyed as Cheston on 800 acres in 1659 for John and William Coursey. Six generations lived and were buried here. The original house burned.

Presquile. The c1820 house overlooks the Wye River and was built by the Lloyd family. Rogers C. B. Morton, U.S. Congressman and Secretary of the Interior once lived here. The house is now owned by the Kimberly Paper Company family.

Bruff's Island. Charles Howard Lloyd built this house in 1888.

The Aspen Institute Wye River Conference Center. The institute was created in 1963 by Arthur A. Houghton, Jr. to bring about economic and social change to this region. Today it continues this tradition, but on a global basis. Most recently it held the Middle East peace talks. The retreat is located on 1,100 acres on the Wye River. Elegant gardens and lovely views of the Wye River surround Houghton House and River House.

Wye Mills

In 1664 Lord Baltimore granted a patent to James Scott for "Old Mill". In 1686 Henrietta Lloyd, widow of Philemon Lloyd, received timber lands from James Scott. "Clover Leaf" was patented to William Helmsburg in 1730 on 1622 acres._

Attractions:

Old Wye Mill. MD Rte. 662. 410-827-6909. The gristmill dates from c1682 and is probably the oldest building still standing in the state and the oldest operating mill. The mill has served as the boundary between Talbot and Queen Anne's Counties since 1706. In 1706 Richard Sweatman operated a sawmill and two gristmills here. Edward Lloyd controlled the mill from 1722 to 1793. Col. William Hemsley operated the mill for Mr. Lloyd and eventually owned it, having married Maria Lloyd, daughter of Edward Lloyd IV. The mill produced cornmeal for Gen. Washington's Continental Army at Valley Forge in 1778. The flour was ordered and paid for by Robert Morris. Alexander Hemsley sold the property to Samuel Hopkins in 1821 for $4,000. During the 1790s Oliver Evans, "Father of the Modern Factory", used the mill for some of his inventions. The state of Maryland eventually bought the mill. It was deeded to the Friends of Wye Mill in 1996. There is only one gristmill operating today still producing meal and flour on the 1st and 3rd Saturday of the month. The mill is listed on the National Register of Historic Places.

Wye Oak State Park is off Route 50. Wye Oak. The oak is the official tree of the state of Maryland. The largest white oak and one of the oldest in the United States was felled during a thunderstorm on June 6, 2002.

Wye Heights. Wye Heights Road. Wye Heights, also known as Cleghorne-on-Wye, is a home built by the Lloyd family in 1823. This private home has magnificent gardens.

Wye School. The building dates c1800 and is thought to be the first public school on the Eastern Shore.

Little House at Wye. On the grounds of the Aspen Institute. In October 1998 the Mid East Summit was held and the Wye River Moratorium signed. The house was renovated in the 1940s after Arthur Houghton, Jr. bought the property. On the grounds are aged boxwood and old oak trees.

Wilton. Private home. The house is located on the remaining five acres of what was once a land grant of 650 acres from Lord Baltimore and patented to Thomas Williams in 1669 and another land grant called "Wilton Addition". The grant included the Wye Grist Mill and the property where the Wye Oak once stood. The property was later owned by the Lloyd and Bennett families and William Hemsley, a member of the Maryland State Senate and Continental Congress. The house was constructed in 1760, with an addition in 1803. The house is listed on the National Register of Historic Places.

Old Wye Church was erected 1717-21 as St. Luke's Wye Chapel for St. Paul's Parish, Centreville. Pews were auctioned off to the highest bidders. This along with one hundred pounds sterling and sixty thousand pounds of tobacco allowed the construction of the church to begin. The silver communion service dates from 1737, and the candlesticks 1692. The vestry house was built in 1761-63 at a cost of $300. Partial restoration of the church was carried out in 1949 through the generosity of Arthur A. Houghton, Jr.

Old Wye Church

Miller's House. The house was constructed in c1750 for Edward Lloyd III.

Pendryn. Private home. The word Pendryn comes from the Welch and means "head of the bird". The house built on the Wye River is a Palladian Georgian house with lovely gardens.

Shopping:

Orrell's Maryland Beaten Biscuits. 410-820-8090

Wye Island

The deed to Wye Island dated 1668 calls it the "Great Island in the Wye River". William Paca, a Signer of the Declaration of Independence and twice Governor of Maryland, built Wye Hall, a large plantation which burned in 1879 on the eastern part of the island. John Beale Bordley, a jurist owned the western part. He also built a plantation with carpentry and blacksmith shops, a ropewalk, brick yard and a brewery. During the American Revolution the island was attacked by a British boat, *The Experiment*.

During the 1970s developers tried to develop the island. Instead the State of Maryland purchased 2,450 acres which is now the Wye Island Natural Resources Management Area.

Copperton

Knightly. This private manor house was built in 1810 as a wedding gift for Edward S. Winder and Elizabeth Tayloe Lloyd, daughter of Edward Lloyd V. Their son, Charles S. Winder became a brigadier general and served under Stonewall Jackson in the Civil War. The house has lovely gardens right down to the creek.

Longwoods

Longwoods has several elegant homes all privately owned.
Myrtle Grove. On Miles River and Goldsborough Creek. Private. Robert Goldsborough of Myrtle Grove, a county justice of the peace, on Goldsborough Creek built this private home in 1724. His son, Robert Goldsborough IV added on to the house in 1790. Mr. Goldsborough was a member of the House of Delegates during the Revolutionary War. He owned 78 slaves at the time of his death. The interior has a three story hanging staircase. On the property is the oldest law office in the United States, a dairy and smoke house. This is a National Trust property.

The Anchorage. Unionville Road. Edward Lloyd V gave this property to his daughter Sarah and her husband, Lt. Charles Lowndes in the 1830s. Charles Lowndes retired from the Navy just before the Civil War, but was a Union sympathizer, unlike the rest of the Lloyd family who were Confederates.

The Rest. The Rest was the home of Ann Catherine Lloyd, also a daughter of Edward Lloyd V. She married Franklin Buchanan, the first Superintendent of the U.S. Naval Academy in Annapolis. He joined the Confederates during the Civil War and commanded the ironclad *Virginia.* He later became the highest ranking officer in the Confederate Navy.

"Ending of the Controversy". This land was granted to Wenlocke Christison in 1670. He had come from Boston where he had been whipped and accused of witchcraft. He was active in the Third Haven Meeting in Easton.

The Little Red Schoolhouse. The school was formerly known as Longwoods Elementary School and was built in 1877. The building was recently renovated and open to the public.

Easton

Easton was settled by Quakers beginning in the early 1660s. A meeting house was built on Job's Cove on the Tred Avon River in 1684. Part of Easton was Cooke's Hope, a land grant given to Major Miles Cooke by the Lord Baron of Baltimore in 1695. Easton was originally called Talbot Court House, later Easton, a contraction of East-town. The two acre piece of land for the court house was situated on Francis Armstrong's 500 acre patent known as London Derry. Mr. Armstrong purchased other property including the 1000 acre Tlghman's Fortune, owned by Captain Samuel Tilghman.

In 1786 legislation was passed to establish the town as Talbot. Easton became the county seat for Talbot County in 1788. Col. Jeremiah Banning, a large landowner in Talbot County, laid out the town and named the streets. John Needles, a silversmith, laid out the lots. It was incorporated in 1790. Much of town was destroyed in fires 1810, 1855 and 1878. Easton Point had a fort to protect Easton during the War of 1812. During the Civil War the citizens had divided loyalties towards the North and South.

The *Republican Star*, later *the Star-Democrat* was established in 1799 and is still published today.

The Maryland and Delaware Railroad began service in 1869. Agricultural products and seafood from the Chesapeake Bay could now be transported to markets outside the Eastern Shore. A number of the Victorian homes in town were built during this period.

In November the Waterfowl Festival, the premier of its kind, attracts people from around the world (410-822-4567).

Attractions:

<u>Easton Welcome & Resource Center</u>. 11 S. Harrison Street. 410-820-8822.The building was constructed in 1827 as a firehouse and remodeled in 1884.

<u>The Third Haven Friends Meeting House.</u> 405 S. Washington Street. The structure was built in 1682, and is the oldest frame building dedicated to religious meetings in the U.S. William Penn preached here with Lord Baltimore present. Renovations were completed in 1990.

<u>Talbot County Courthouse</u>. 11 North Washington Street. The first courthouse was built in 1710-12 by Philemon Hemsley. The present one dates from 1794, with several wings added after that date. The "Talbot Resolves" were adopted here, and later incorporated into the Declaration of Independence. On July 31,

1783 five Masonic Lodges met here to form the first Grand Lodge of Masons in Maryland.

Bullitt House. 108 Dover Street. The house was built 1801 by Thomas Bullitt, and is now the Mid-Shore Community Foundation.

Jump House. 107 Goldsborough Street. This late 19th c home in the Queen Anne style was built for the Jump family, who ran a large dry goods store in Easton.

The Historical Society of Talbot County. 25 South Washington Street. 410-822-0773. The museum features changing exhibitions on local history and has an elegant garden. The garden wall design is a duplicate of the cemetery wall at Wye House. And the picket fence after the one at the Hammond-Harwood House in Annapolis. Free garden concerts are given May-September.

The Society maintains the James Neall House built c1810 for James Neall, a Quaker cabinetmaker and his wife Rachael,

James Neall House

Foxley Hall. North Aurora and Goldsborough Streets. This was built c1795 by Mrs. Henry Dickinson. Later it was the home of U.S. Senator John Leeds Kerr who named it Burnside. Dr. Samuel A. Harrison remodeled the house for his daughter Patty Belle and her husband, Oswald Tilghman, who named it Foxley Hall. Dr. Harrison and Mr. Tilghman wrote the two-volume *History of Talbot County*.

Gross' Coate Plantation 1658. 11300 Gross' Coate Road. Private. This plantation is on a tract granted by Lord Baltimore to Roger Gross in 1658. Later the Tilghman family purchased the property.

Hughlett Henry House. 26 South Street. This house was built c 1795

Hambleton. 28 South Harrison Street. In 1790 Benjamin Stevens purchased 3 lots in Easton. This Georgian building dates c 1794, the year Stevens died. Samuel Hambleton, a lawyer, purchased the building in 1845.

Bishop's House. 214 Goldsborough Street. This house was built for Philip Francis Thomas, U.S. Congressman, Maryland Governor, and Secretary of the Treasury under President Buchanan. The house dates c1880.

Bruff/Hollyday House. 113 North Washington. This house is c1791.

Saint Aubens. 105 Willis Avenue. This 1803 house was once part of a large farm in Easton.

6 North Washington Street. This house was built c1795 by Lambert Hopkins who had purchased the property in 1785.

Thomas Perrin Smith House. 119 N. Washington Street. The founder of the newspaper, today known as the Easton-Star Democrat built the house in 1803. The building is now the Chesapeake Bay Yacht Club.

Stewart Building. North Washington Street. This was once the Old Brick Hotel and was built c1810.

The Old Market House. Harrison Street and Magazine Alley. This building was erected in 1791. The first meetings of the Grand Lodge of Maryland of the Masonic Order were held here in 1783.

Academy Art Museum. 106 South Street. 410-822-ARTS. Famous American artists are represented here. Classes and concerts are also given in the building which dates to the mid 1800s.

Christ Church. 111 South Harrison Street. The church was founded in 1692, and is the fifth place of worship for St. Peter's Parish. The present building was built 1840-45 of Port Deposit granite.

Ashby 1663. Ashby Drive. Private. This is one of the most elegant homes on the Eastern Shore, dating back to 1663.

Ashby 1663

Talbot Free Library. James Michener's proofs and other memorabilia were given to the library after he spent much time using the Maryland Room for his research for "Chesapeake"

Trinity Cathedral. Goldsborough Street. The Cathedral is the headquarters of the Episcopal Diocese of Easton, which covers the nine counties of the Eastern Shore. The building was consecrated in 1894.

Avalon Theater. 40 E. Dover Street. 410-822-0345. The building was constructed c1922. The theater has presented outstanding shows and performers, and was the scene of three world premiers included "The First Kiss", starring Fay Wray and Gary Cooper in 1928, filmed in St. Michael's.

Talbot County Country Club. 6142 Country Club Road. The club is on property once owned by Richard Tilghman Goldsborough called Llandaff.

Turner's Point. This property was granted to William Turner, a Quaker, in 1663. Later Thomas Skillington built ships on the property.

Ratcliffe Manor. In 1920 Malcolm Hathaway, son of the owners of Ratcliffe, constructed a flying field. He and his partner Robins Hollyday established an aerial photography business.

207 Harrison Street. Private home. The house was built in the 1890s for the Nevins family. It is typical of many of the Victorian style homes in Easton.

211 S. Harrison Street. Private home. The house was built for Senator and Mrs. Harry Covington in 1911. Sen. Covington served in the U.S. Senate from 1908-14.

213 S. Harrison Street. The house was built in 1908 for Judge Mason Shehan.

Pickering Creek Environmental Center. 11450 Audubon Lane. 410-822-4903. 400 acre preserve.

Bellevue Cemetery. Members of the Bozman family are buried here.

Spring Hill Cemetery. North and Hanson Streets. The land was purchased in 1802 and in 1827 a plot was given by Dr. Ennals Martin to Christ Church to be used as a cemetery. In 1847 the Methodist Church purchased a lot near Christ Church. These two plots were joined in 1877.

Shannahan & Wrightson Hardware Building. Dover and Washington Streets. The oldest store in Easton was built in 1791 by Owen Kennard. Additions were made in 1877, 1881 and 1889. The front was completed on December 7, 1941, Pearl Harbor Day. Today the building is the Court House Square Shops.

First Masonic Grand Lodge. Washington Street. Five Masonic lodges met here on July 31,1783 to form the first Grand Lodge of Masons in Maryland.

Talbot County Women's Club. The building dates back to the 18th. It was bought by the club in 1943 and restored.

Easton Memorial Hospital. Washington Street. The hospital was built in 1907.

Captain Clement Vickers House. Ocean Gateway. This small house was built c1800 by ship captain Clement Vickers and moved to its present location in 1968.

Easton Airport. Rte. 50. The airport was built in 1939 with very long runways as an interceptor airport for the impending World War II. Today the airport attracts biplanes, private jets and smaller planes.

White Marsh Church. Just south of Easton on Rte. 50 lie the ruins of White Marsh Church. The original church was built between 1662-65, although the first date mentioned in parish records is 1690 when Joseph Leeds was acting rector. This was designated as one of the original 30 parishes in 1692. Rev. Thomas Bacon served as rector 1746-68. He wrote "Laws of Maryland at Large" in 1765. The church was remodeled in 1751 Services after 1795 alternated between Easton, the county seat and Whitemarsh. In 1847 the rector moved to the new Christ Church in Easton. The church was abandoned during the Civil War, and burned in 1896. Robert Morris Senior, who died in 1750, is buried here.

Millwood. Oxford Road. Private home. This was once part of the Harleigh estate located on Trippe Creek. The house was built in the 1830s with additions afterwards.

Jena. Oxford Road. Private home. The house could have been built as early as 1673. The owner Jacob Gibson named it for one of the Napoleonic battles. The house is one of a few telescope houses located on the Eastern Shore.

"Boston Cliff'. Private. The house just south of Easton on the Choptank River was patented in 1665. The first part of the house was built in c1674 and the second in 1729.

Lodging:

Tidewater Inn and Conference Center. 11 East Dover Street. 410-822-1300. The inn replaced the 1890 Avon Hotel destroyed by fire in 1944 and was built in 1949at the cost of $1.25 million and enlarged in 1953. The Inn was recently sold and extensive renovations have taken place.
The Inn at Easton. 28 South Harrison Street. 410-822-4910. The house was built by Benjamin Stevens in 1790. It is one of the earliest three-bay brick buildings on the Eastern Shore.
Easton's Promise. 107 Goldsborough Street. 410-820-9159
John S. McDaniel House. 14 N. Aurora Street. 410-822-3704. Built 1890. Each floor has a turret.
Bishop's House. 214 Goldsborough Street. 410-820-7290. Built for Philip Francis Thomas, governor of Maryland 1848-51. In 1892 sold to Episcopal Church and was the residence of the Bishop of the Diocese of Easton.
Miles River Guest House. 888-561-5930
Chaffinch House B&B. 132 S. Harrison Street. 800-861-5074
Comfort Inn. 8523 Ocean Gateway. 410-820-8333

Days Inn. 7018 Ocean Gateway. 410-822-4600
Holiday Inn Express. 8561 Ocean Gateway. 410-819-6500
Econo Lodge. 8175 Ocean Gateway. 410-820-5555

Restaurants:

Restaurant Columbia. 28 South Washington Street. 410-770-5172. The restaurant is located in a c1795 home.
The Inn at Easton. 28 South Harrison Street. 410-822-4910
The Tidewater Grill. Dover and Harrison Streets. 410-822-1300
Mason's. 22 Harrison Street. 410-822-3204
Eagle Spirits at the Easton Club. 28449 Clubhouse Drive. 410-820-4100
Out of the Fire Café and Wine Bar. 22 Goldsborough Street. 410-770-4777
Chez Lafite. 13 S. Washington Street. 410-770-8868
Martinis Restaurant. 28449 Clubhouse Drive. 410-820-4100
Rustic Inn of Easton. Talbottown on Harrison Street. 410-820-8212
Legal Spirits. 42 E. Dover Street. 410-820-0033
Olde Towne Creamery. 9B Goldsborough Street. 410-820-5223
GeneralKanuki's Restaurant. 25 Goldsborough Street. 410-819-0707
Out of the Fire. 22 Goldsborough Street. 410-770-4777
Portofino Ristorante Italiano. 4 W. Dover Street. 410-770-9200
Washington Street Pub. 20 N. Washington Street. 410-822-9011
Sweet Nina's Italian Treats. 37 E. Dover Street. 410-763-9272
Crystal Café. 201 Marlboro Avenue. 410-822-2224
The Kitchen. 22A N. Harrison Street. 410-819-6780
Hangar Café. Easton Airport. 410-820-6631
Fiddle Leaf Café. 12 W. Dover Street. 410-822-4353
Peach Blossoms. 6 N. Washington Street. 410-822-5220
Tom's Tavern. A Steakhouse. N. West Street. 410-770-3710.
Yesteryear's. Easton Plaza. 410-822-2433
Jin Jin Chinese Restaurant. 6 N. Washington Street. 410-820-0011
House of Hunan. 201 A Marlboro Road. 410-820-4015
H&G. Rt. 50. 410-822-1085. A favorite hangout
Railway Market. 108 Marlboro Street. 410-822-4852
Coffee East. 5 Goldsborough Street. 410-819-6711
G&H Seafood Market. Dover and Aurora Streets. 410-820-7364. Carry-out
Pepper Jack's Mexican. Rte. 50 East. 410-819-0582
Timeout Tap & Grill. Easton Marketplace. 410-820-0433
Guiffrida's Pizza. 810 Dover Road. 410-819-3296
Old Mill Deli. 1021 N. Main Street. 410-822-9613
Courthouse Square Deli. 12 N. Washington Street. 410-820-7950
Downtown Desserts & Café. 32 N. Washington Street. 410-822-8996
Hill's Soda Fountain. 32 E. Dover Street. 410-822-2666
Chilaquiles. 12 W. Dover Street. 410-770-9660
Zambrino's. 606 Dover Road. 410-822-4911

Alice's Café. 22 N. Harrison Street. 410-819-8590
Alice's Café. 12 W. Dover Street. 410-770-5831. Cakes and desserts

Royal Oak

The town probably received its name from a large oak tree that was hit by cannonballs during the siege of St. Michael's in 1813 by the British.

Attractions:

Orem's Delight. John Morris purchased Fox Hole in 1676 from William Smythe. His grandson, Morris Orem built the c1725 house.

Belle Aire. Rte. 33. This gracious home was built in 1788. Private home.

Lodging:

The Oaks: A Country Inn. 25876 Royal Oak Road. 410-745-5053. This gracious home was built in 1748 and sits on 17 waterfront acres.
Royal Oak House B&B. 410-745-3025

Dining:

Bella Luna Italian Market. 25942 Royal Oak Road. 410-745-6100

Bellevue

A ferry has crossed the Tred Avon River here since 1760, the first run by Elizabeth Skinner. The ferry is unattached to a cable and crosses to Oxford.

William Collins, Jr. purchased sixty acres of land from the owners of Clay's Hope in the late 19th c. He sold a half interest to Oswald Tilghman and together they planned to develop a resort on the Tred Avon River. The area was called "Bellevue" for Mr. Tilghman's wife, Belle Harrison Tilghman, daughter of Dr. Samuel A. Harrison who had been born at Clay's Hope. Mr. Collins and Mr. Tilghman began to sell some of the property in 1883. Both white and black families bought land due to the fact that many of the African-American families were prospering in the oyster shucking business. Mr. Tilghman eventually bought out Mr. Collins. William H. Valliant bought six acres and started a canning and packing company that eventually employed 200 employees. Other property was sold to William Dawson. Dawson and Valliant were to build homes which they rented to the workers.

In 1937 Samuel Aubrey Turner, son of one of the first black schooner captains started his own oyster business, W. A. Turner & Sons. Following World War II his son, Samuel Edward Turner formed the Bellevue Seafood Company. He also built workboats.

St. Luke United Methodist Church. This church was founded when the black Methodists from Ferry Neck and Deep Neck churches united in 1882. The chapel was completed in 1903.

St. Michael's

St. Michael's was settled in 1677. The town was named for St. Michael the Archangel. William Hambleton of Martingham named the river Myles in 1675. St. Michael's had several lands grants, among them "The Beach", a fifty acre tract, that includes the present harbor in 1644. "Stauper", also fifty acres, was granted in 1667 to Christopher Stauper. This ran from the Miles River to Back Creek. "Davenport", the present site of Perry Cabin was granted in 1675. The area was noted for shipbuilding and the growing of tobacco.

In 1770 an Englishman, James Braddock, purchased land and laid it out in lots. St. Michael's was incorporated in 1804, surveyed and laid out in three squares. In 1805 a central area was set aside for the public market house, St. Mary's Square. On the square is the ship's carpenter's bell cast in 1841 that rang at 7AM, noon and 5PM to measure the workday for the ships' carpenters who worked in the nearby shipyards.

During the War of 1812, on August 10, 1813, the townspeople being forewarned of a British attack, hoisted lanterns in treetops and on ship's masts. The town was blacked out, and the British fired, missing all but one home, now known as "The Cannonball House". St. Michael's became known as "The Town that fooled the British".

About 1820 when the supply of lumber was depleted, shipbuilding became centered in Baltimore. In 1829 with the opening of the Chesapeake and Delaware Canal oystering became a major livelihood. For many years St. Michael's also was a harvesting and processing center for seafood. Navy Point was subdivided into town lots in 1851. Until that time it had been part of Perry Cabin. The first railroad was built in 1890, bringing in tourists to enjoy this lovely town. Later smaller types of boats were constructed.

The author James Michener lived on Church Neck overlooking Broad Creek from 1977 to 1983 while he researched and wrote "Chesapeake". He never returned and his house was sold in 1996. Some of his neighbors included Sen. George McGovern and Graham Kerr, the "Galloping Gourmet". Harold Baines of St. Michael's played for the Baltimore Orioles. A picture of him hangs in the Court House in Easton.

Attractions:

St. Michael's has many historic homes, shops and a beautiful harbor. A good walking tour map is available.

St. Mary's Square. The square was laid out in 1770 by James Braddock. It has lovely homes and St. Mary's Square Museum, a 19th c home of "half timber" structure. The site was originally patented to John Hollingsworth in 1659.

Cannonball House – Mulberry Street and St. Mary's Square. Only home damaged by the British during the War of 1812. This c 1805 house was built by shipwright William Marchant.

Tarr House. Built c 1661 by Edward Elliott as his plantation. Mr. Elliott and his indentured servant, Darby Coghorn built the first church in St. Michael's about 1677, on the site of the present Episcopal Church (6 Willow Street).

Higgins House. The house was built 1854-55 and today is part of the Chesapeake Bay Maritime Museum.

Bruff House. The house is located on land sold to John Bruff in 1791 for 20 pounds and remained in his family until the mid 1900's.

Amelia Welby House. Built 1700's from brick and now covered in mahogany siding. This was once the home of the first "Poet Laureate of Maryland".

The Footbridge. The bridge joins Navy Point to Cherry Street. Over the years many bridges have been built here. It has also been called the Honeymoon Bridge and Sweetheart Bridge.

Frederick Douglass Historic Marker. Frederick Douglass was born at Tuckahoe Creek, but lived as a slave in St. Michael's from 1833-36. He taught himself to read and taught in nearby schools. He escaped to the north and became the noted abolitionist.

Hooper Strait Lighthouse

Chesapeake Bay Maritime Museum- Mill Street. 410-822-3456. The museum, founded in 1965, has many wonderful boats, models, decoys and other maritime related items. This was once the site of crab picking and processing plants. The Hooper Strait Lighthouse built in 1879 and the Knapp's Narrows Bridge have been moved to the museum grounds. The bridge is a bascule bridge, weighing 108 tons. The Museum bought it from the state for $1.
Recently the museum renovated several houses located on its property. They include the Dodson House which was built in the late 1800s for a local shopkeeper. Richard Stearns Dodson began to acquire properties on Navy Point in the 1880s which he renovated and rented to summer visitors. The house remained in the Dodson family until 1907 and then was repurchased in 1912. The museum acquired the house in 1963 and in 1964 the Higgins and Eagle houses.

"The Cottage". Original home of shipwright Robert Lambdin and his descendants 1840 to 1905.

"The Old Inn". Talbot Street at Mulberry. Built c 1816 by Wrightson Jones, who owned and operated the shipyard at Beverly on Broad Creek.

Mill House. Harrison Square. The house was originally built on the beach c 1660, and later moved.

Christ Episcopal Church. 301 S. Talbot Street. The church was erected in 1878 of Port Deposit stone on the site of a church built by Edward Elliott. During the Revolutionary War, the rector, Rev. John Gordon, was one of the few to maintain a parish of the Church of England He served here from 1749 to 1790. The harbor once came up to this property. The land is now filled.

Christ Church

Perry Hall. Perry Hall was built by John Rogers and his wife Maria Perry c 1820 and was the site of the 1998 Eastern Shore Designer Showhouse. The house is owned by the Marine Engineer's Beneficial Association (MEBA) and sits on 350 acres.

Freedom's Friend Lodge. This lodge for African Americans was chartered in 1867 and is the oldest in existence in Maryland.

Hell's Crossing. Where Locust and Carpenter Streets crossed was called "Hell's Crossing" and "Racket Alley" due to the noise from the shipyards and fog bell.

Beverly. On San Domingo Creek. The Harper family built this house in 1853-57. It once was a plantation of 1500 acres and had a small boatyard. Private home.

"Beverly"
Photo courtesy of Jean Harper Baer

Martingham. Robert Martyn received a tract of 500 acres in the mid 17th c. 200 acres of the original tract was assigned to William Hambleton of Scotland. He was a sheriff of Talbot County by 1663 and justice of the peace. A descendant, Samuel Hambleton, born at Martingham in 1777, served as purser of the U.S. Navy and under Comm. Perry at the Battle of Lake Erie.

Sherwood Manor Farm. This was once part of a larger farm named "Sherwood Manor" and dates from 1713. On the farm is a walnut tree dating back over 200 years.

"Crooked Intention". Private. Hugh Sherwood was granted a patent in 1681 for a tract of 130 acres at the headwaters of San Domingo Creek. He named the patent "Crooked Intention". In 1691 he sold 50 acres to Robert Harrison. His son also named Robert built the one and one half story brick building. The Harrisons were to become successful merchants and shipbuilders and changed the name of the property to "Canton Farm" The property was purchased by Mr. and Mrs. G.A. Van Lennep, Jr. in 1946 and changed the name back to "Crooked Intention".

The Thomas Harrison House. 201 Green Street. This c 1790 house is on the harbor.

Sunset Cottage. Carpenter Street. Private. The house was built c1805 and moved from Freemont Street in 2002. The wooden rafters are made from old skipjack and log canoes.

Miles River Yacht Club. The club was organized in 1920. The club is dedicated to preserving the log canoes and sponsors races during the summer.

Lodging:

Inn at Perry Cabin. 308 Watkins Lane. 410-745-2200. This elegant inn on the Miles River was owned by the Laura Ashley family and sold in 1999 to Orient-Express Hotels, Inc. of London. The original house was built in the 19th c by Samuel Hambleton, a purser in the United States Navy during the War of 1812. The house was named for his friend, Commodore Oliver Hazzard Perry. During the 1920s Charles H. Fogg, owner and operator of coal mines and coke ovens in Pennsylvania enlarged the house. The Gary Cooper and Fay Wray movie *The First Kiss* was filmed here. The inn was recently added on to and extensive renovations were made.
St. Michael's Harbour Inn & Marina. 101 N. Harbor Road. 410-745-9001. right on harbor downtown.
Harbourtowne Golf Resort and Conference Center. Rte. 33 at Martingham Drive. 410-745-9066. Located on Miles River.
Five Gables Inn & Spa. 209 N. Talbot Street. 410-745-0100.
Parsonage Inn. 210 N. Talbot Street. 410-745-5519. The house was built in 1883 by Henry Clay Dodson, a St. Michael's businessman and legislator. Mr. Dodson and Joseph White founded the St. Michael's Brick Company.
Victoriana Inn. 205 Cherry Street. 410-745-3368. The house was built in 1873 by Dr. Clay Dodson, a U.S. army officer during the Civil War. In 1910 the Shannahan family bought property and named it "Willow Cottage". It was restored in 1988 as a B&B.
Kemp House Inn. 412 S. Talbot Street. 410-745-2243. Georgian built 1805 for Col. Joseph Kemp, a revolutionary soldier and War of 1812 hero.

Dr. Dodson House B&B. 200 Cherry Street. 410-745-3691. This c1799 brick house was originally a tavern.
The Fleet's Inn. 200 E. Chew Street. 410-745-9678
Hambleton Inn. 202 Cherry Street. 410-745-3350. The waterfront house was built in 1860. The property has dockage for boats up to 32 feet.
Rigby Valliant House B&B. 123 W. Chestnut Street. 410-745-3977. A c 1832 house.
Snuggery Guest House. 203 Cherry Street. 410-745-2800. Harbor view
Tarr House B&B. 109 Green Street. 410-745-2175. One of St. Michael's oldest houses.
Captain's Quarters. 115 E. Chew Avenue. 410-745-9152
Two Swan Inn. 208 Carpenter Street. 410-745-2929. The house was built in 1790 and served as the former site of the Miles River Yacht Club.
The Old Brick Inn. 401 S. Talbot Street. 410-743-3323
Barrett's Bed & Breakfast Inn. 204 N. Talbot Street. 410-745-3322
Harris Cove Cottages Bed 'N Boat. 8080 Bozman-Neavitt Road. 410-745-9701
Best Western St. Michael's Motor Inn. 1228 S. Talbot Street. 410-745-3333
Broad Creek B&B. 8764 Mount Pleasant Landing Court. 410-745-6811
George Brooks House B&B. 24500 Rolles Range Road. 410-745-0999

Wade's Point Inn

Wades Point Inn on the Bay. Wade's Point. 410-745-2500. Named for Zachary Wade who received a land grant in 1657. Thomas Kemp, the original builder of

the "Pride of Baltimore", built the 1819 farmhouse. This is one of the most beautiful inns on the Eastern Shore with views of the Bay and up the Miles River.
Adams Water Chestnut Cottage. 417 Water Street. 410-745-6770
Bay Cottage B&B. 24640 Yacht Club Road. 888-558-8008
Cherry Street Inn. 103 Cherry Street. 410-745-6309
Folly's Cove B&B. 24811 Ray's Point Road. 410-745-5515
The Getaway B&B. Long Haul Creek. 877-363-8236

Dining:

Crab Claw Restaurant. Navy Point. 410-745-2900. A favorite spot right on the water next to the Chesapeake Bay Maritime Museum. Takes only cash.
208 Talbot. 208 N. Talbot Street. 410-745-3838. Serves dinner and Sunday brunch
Sherwood Landing at the Inn at Perry Cabin. 410-745-2200. The inn serves excellent meals and afternoon tea.
St. Michael's Crab House. 305 Mulberry Street. 410-745-3737
Carpenter Street Saloon. 113 S. Talbot Street. 410-745-5111. The tavern was built in 1874, and has served as a bank, newspaper office, post office, and telephone company.
Pascal's Tavern. St. Michael's Harbour Inn & Marina. 101 N. Harbor Road. 410-745-9001
Harbour Lights. St. Michael's Harbour Inn & Marina. 101 N. Harbor Road. 410-745-5102
Town Dock Restaurant. 125 Mulberry Street. 410-745-5577. During the War of 1812 this was known as Dawson's Wharf. In the 1950's "The Longfellow Inn" was on this site. It burned, and the present building was constructed in 1977.
Key Lime Cafe. 207 N. Talbot Street. 410-745-3158
Justine's. 106 N. Talbot. Old fashioned ice cream parlor
Bistro St. Michael's. 403 S. Talbot Street, 410-745-9111
Yesteryear"s Food & Spirits. 200 S. Talbot Street. 410-745-6206
Barrett's Tea Room. 204 N. Talbot Street. 410-745-3322. Tea served daily
Blue Crab Coffee Company. 102 Fremont Street. 410-745-4155
Characters Café. 200 S. Talbot. Street. 410-745-6206
Foxy's Marina Bar. 125 Mulberry Street. 410-745-4340
Gourmet by the Bay. 415 South Talbot Street. 410-745-6260
Tavern on Talbot. 409 S. Talbot Street. 866-309-9343
Big Al's Market. 302 N. Talbot Street. 410-745-3151
The Village Shoppe. 501 Talbot Street. 410-745-9300

Furniture Restoration:

McMartin & Beggins. 410-745-5715

Special Events:

Log Canoe Racing started in St. Michael's 1840-60 on Miles River and is being raced again in canoes many over a 100 years old. The canoes were once used to gather food, harvest shellfish and for transportation by the Indians. They are a sight to behold. Races are held throughout the summer.

Other events include the Classic and Antique Boat Show in June, and Concerts in the Park June to August.

Claiborne

Claiborne was named for William Claiborne who settled on Kent Island. The Baltimore and Eastern Shore Railroad established the village in 1866 as a ferry point between Baltimore and the Eastern Shore.

Webley. Just south of Claiborne on Rte. 33 is the house purchased by Dr. Absalom Thompson in 1826. He converted the house into the first hospital on the Eastern Shore.

Rich Neck Manor. Rich Neck Manor was patented to Col. Henry Fox in 1649. Samuel Harrison, a lawyer, built the present house c1824.

Lodging:

Maple Hall. 23253 Maple Hall Road. 410-745-2673

McDaniel

Dining:

Chesapeake Landing. Rte. 33. 410-745-9600. Steaks and seafood

Pot Pie

Pot Pie sterned boats were originally built on Harris' Creek.

Bozman

The town is named for the Bozman family. John Leeds Bozman, an attorney and historian, wrote one of the early histories of Maryland. "The History of Maryland from Its First Settlement, in 1633, to the Restoration in 1660, with a Copious Introduction, and Notes and Illustrations" was published in Baltimore in 1837.

Lostock. This property was surveyed for John Anderton in 1659. Lostock was built by Major William Caulk in the late 18th c.

Attractions:

Jean Ellen duPont Sheehan Audubon Sanctuary. 23000 Wells Point Road. 410-745-9283

Lodging:

Grandview Rentals. 6601 Bozman Neavitt Road. 866-392-4876
Ben's Woods B&B. 8063 Bozman-Neavitt Road. 410-745-4051

Sherwood

Lodging:

The Moorings B&B. Rte. 33. 410-745-6396
Lowes Wharf Marina Inn. 21651 Lowes Wharf Road. 410-745-6684

Wittman

Lodging:

Watermark B&B. 8956 Tilghman Island Road. 410-745-2892
The Inn at Christmas Farm. 8873 Tilghman Island Road. 410-745-5312

Tilghman Island

Tilghman Island Church decorated for Christmas

Tilghman is an out of the way, but in a lovely Eastern Shore setting, where many of the families have lived in the same houses for generations. Separated from the Eastern Shore by the Knapps Narrows, it was once called Choptank Island.

Tilghman was first charted by John Smith in 1608. The island was first surveyed for Seth Foster in 1659 when he began to cultivate the land. In 1662 the Talbot County Court was established with Seth Foster as a Commissioner. When he died he owned over 2,000 acres of land.

One hundred fifty acres were claimed by Robert Knapp in Kent County, but he later acquired land near Choptank Island. Knapp's Narrows is named for him. At the time of the Talbot County Court he took the oath of Constable.

The island then passed on to several other families and in 1697 the Coursey's of Talbot County sold it to John Hawkins who began to develop it and brought in slaves. In 1724 Col. Matthew Tilghman Ward who married Margaret Lloyd of Wye bought the island. The island was divided into four plantations. In Mr. Ward's will in 1741 he gave his cousin Matthew Tilghman all of Choptank Island. Matthew Tilghman was only 23 and was to marry Anna Maria Lloyd. Their daughters - Anna Maria married her first cousin Tench Tilghman and Margaretta married Charles Carroll. Mr. Tilghman was known as the "Patriarch of Maryland". He was speaker of the Assembly which appointed the delegation to the Continental Congress in Philadelphia and presided over Maryland's first constitutional convention.

During the War of 1812 a number of men from Tilghman joined the 26th Regiment of the Maryland Militia. Today many of those families still live on Tilghman including the Fairbanks (Fairbank Tackle), Larrimores (Captain Stanley Larrimore), Harrisons (Harrison's Chesapeake House), Lowerys (Maynard Lowery boat builder), and a number of other families. Black Walnut Cove was for a while called Barney's Cove, named for Commodore Joshua Barney.

All the slaves were freed and their housing turned over to the watermen. In 1842 the island was sold to Tench Tilghman, grandson of Washington's aide-de-camp, for $24,000 also. In 1842 John Valliant paid $4000 for 150 acres in the southern part of the Lower Plantation. This is now the Black Walnut Point Inn. Tench Tilghman built the first bridge across the Narrows. In 1846 James Seth bought all the remaining land owned by Tench Tilghman.

Choptank Island was purchased in 1838 by Dr. Absalom Thompson for $24,000.

Tilghman Island was one of the main places for oystering on the Chesapeake. In 1897 the Tilghman Packing plant was opened by the Harrison family and closed in 1977. The skipjack became the most successful boat for dredging oysters.

The bridge across the Narrows was the longest single span drawbridge in Maryland and was built in 1934 (now at Chesapeake Maritime Museum in St. Michael's). A new bridge was built to replace it in 1998.

Tilghman Island is home to some of the last skipjacks (oyster boats) on the Chesapeake. The *H.M. Krentz*, owned by Ed Farley and the *Rebecca T. Ruark*, owned by Capt. Wade H. Murphy, Jr. still dredge oysters, and during the off-oyster season takes passengers for trips around the Bay. Other types of boats including catboats are still built here.

Tilghman has three villages- Tilghman, Barneck and Fairbank.

Maynard Lowery Catboat in Knapps Narrows

Attractions:

Tilghman Island Trail. A guide for non-powered water vessels can be obtained by calling 410-770-8000.

Lodging:

The Tilghman Island Inn. Coopertown Road. 410-886-2141
The Inn at Knapp's Narrows. 6176 Tilghman Island Road. 1-800-322-5181
Harrison's Country Inn & Sportfishing. 21551 Chesapeake House Drive. 410-886-2121
Black Walnut Point Inn. Black Walnut Road. 410-886-2452
Crosswinds. 21642 Jackson Point Road. 410-886-2826
Sinclair House. 5718 Black Walnut Point Road. 410-886-2147
Chesapeake Wood Duck Inn. Dogwood Harbor. 800-956-2070
Lazyjack Inn. Dogwood Harbor. 410-886-2215
Island Home. 5918 Tilghman Island Road. 410-886-2454
The Jackson House on Tilghman Island. 21483 Mission Road. 410-745-6772

Restaurants:

Tilghman Island Inn. 410-886-2141

Harrison's Chesapeake House. 410-886-2121
So Neat Café & Bakery. 5772 Tilghman Island Road. 410-886-2143
Bay One Hundred. Rte. 33 and Knapps Narrows. 410-886-2126
The Bridge Restaurant. Knapps Narrows. 410-886-2330

Poplar Island

Off Tilghman Island are several islands - Poplar, Jefferson and Coach. William Claiborne of Kent Island explored the Bay in 1626-27 and named Poplar Island Popeley's Island for an associate of his. In 1635 he granted the island to his cousin Richard Thompson. Thompson and his family were killed by Native Americans in 1637. Alexander D'Hinoyossa, the director of the Dutch settlements in Delaware, came to Maryland in 1644 after the British captured New Amstel (now New Castle), and purchased Poplar Island in 1699.

In 1847 Charles Carroll the grandson of Charles Carroll of Carrollton raised black cats here to send pelts to China. A long cold winter caused the ice to freeze and a natural bridge allowed the cats to escape to the mainland. Much of the island eroded over the years, but today the U.S. Army Corps of Engineers is involved in the $427 million Poplar Island project. Using soil dredged from the Chesapeake Bay they are restoring the island, which will become a 1,100 acre wildlife refuge.

Oxford

Oxford was settled c 1635 and had two names – Thread Haven and Third Haven. In 1668 thirty acres were set aside for the town. The town was founded in 1683 and used as a Port of Entry in 1694, along with Anne Arundel (Annapolis). At that time there was an attempt to make Oxford capital of the colony. The name was briefly changed to Williamstadt, in honor of King William. It was incorporated 1706 and eventually became a haven for Quakers and Arcadians who emigrated from Canada. Oxford was once Maryland's largest port, but now has a population of less than 800.

The Oxford-Bellevue ferry has been operating since 1683, either as a scow propelled by sail, or by other means. Today the ferry is the oldest, non-cable ferry in the United States. It is just an easy hop over to St. Michael's, unless you want to drive around.

Lt. Col. Tench Tilghman, an important Revolutionary War hero is buried at the Oxford Cemetery. He was General Washington's aide-de-camp and personal secretary and carried news of the British surrender at Yorktown to the Continental Congress. Col. Tilghman was one of the first people to use the Hussey reaper developed by Obed Hussey of Union Town, Maryland. Plimhimmon, the Tilghman family home dates from a land grant in 1659.

The replica of the customhouse stands next to the Tred Avon Yacht Club on the Strand and was originally located on the other side of the Tred Avon. After the Revolution Oxford lost its importance as a port, and tobacco was no longer shipped from here. The railroad arrived in 1871 stimulating growth of the seafood processing business. By the 1880's steamboats brought visitors who stayed along The Strand.

Oxford Dinghy

Today Oxford remains a boat building center. There are few oyster boats left, but oystering and crabbing are still important. Oxford is a delightful town, has many lovely old buildings, and during the summer is a favorite stop for yachtsmen.

Attractions:

Academy House. 205 N. Morris Street. This was an officers' residence for the Maryland Military Academy 1845-55, the preparatory school for the Naval Academy, which was established under the sponsorship of Tench Tilghman. The house is also known as the Bratt Mansion and is a fine example of the Greek revival style, built in 1848.

Plimhimmon. MD Rte. 333. This private property was purchased by John Coward in 1719. In 1786 Matthew Tilghman bought Plimhimmon and gave it to his daughter, Anna Maria, the widow of George Washington's aide-de-camp, Col. Tench Tilghman. She willed the house to Gen. Tench Tilghman. He built the first steam-powered sawmills on Tilghman Island in the 1850's. His son, also Tench, became an aid to Jefferson Davis during the Civil War.

Oxford Cemetery. This was once part of Plimhimmon.

Tench Tilghman Monument. Oxford Cemetery on Rte. 333. Tench Tilghman and his wife Anna Marie Tilghman are buried in the cemetery.

Oxford-Bellevue Ferry. N. Morris Street and The Strand. This is believed to be the oldest privately operated ferry in U.S. operating since 1683. The first keeper was Richard Royston.

Oxford Museum. Morris and Market Streets. Open Friday and Saturday afternoons or by appointment. Contains Oxford memorabilia.
The Strand. The road along the Tred Avon River has many lovely homes.

Barnaby House. 212 N. Morris Street. The house was built in 1770 by Capt. Richard Barnaby, a sea captain and is listed in the National Register of Historic Places.

Oxford Custom House. N. Morris Street. This building was built in 1976 and is a replica of 18th c customs house used by Jeremiah Banning, the first federal collector of customs appointed by George Washington.

408 S. Morris Street. Private home. The was built in 1900 for John Faulkner, the lighthouse keeper at Benoni Point.

214 S. Morris Street. The c1876 is known as the Fairwinds or Stewart Cooper House.

The Parsonage. 212 S. Morris Street. The house was built in 1870 as the parsonage for the Methodist church.

Byberry & Calico. On the grounds of Cutts & Case Boatyard, Byberry is one of the oldest houses in Oxford dating to c1695. The house was originally located in town and was moved to its present site about 1930.

Grapevine House. 309 N. Morris Street. Private. Captain William Willis, who commanded the brig *Sarah and Louisa*, brought the grapevine in the front from the Isle of Jersey in 1810.

The Oxford Community Center. 200 Oxford Road. 410-226-5904. Classes, lectures, performances and art shows are held in this building.

Oxford Library. 101 Market Street. The library was founded in 1939 and has been at this site since 1952.

Downes F. Curtis Sail Loft. Curtis Downes was a renowned African-American sailmaker who lived in Oxford. The sail loft was originally a schoolhouse for African-Americans built in 1899. It went from grades one to eighth grade. It was closed in the 1930's. Mr. Curtis' mother taught at the school and all nine children were educated there. The Talbot County Board of education sold the property in 1944 to Nellie and Albert Wilson, owners of an ice cream parlor. This building they turned into a restaurant for workers in the nearby oyster shucking and crab picking houses.

Mr. Curtis learned the art of sailmaking from an Englishman, Dave Pritchett. He died in 1936 and Mr. Curtis' brother, Albert, joined the business. They rented the upper floor of the schoolhouse and ran the sail loft there until Downes Curtis' death in 1996 at age 85. Albert died the same year. In January 2001 Nellie Wilson Leatherberry put the property up for sale. Ward Bucher, a restoration architect, and his wife Lisa Johnson bought the property and have restored the sail loft.

The Tred Avon Yacht Club. N. Morris and the Strand. The club was founded in 1931 and the present building completed in 1990.

Lodging:

Robert Morris House Inn. 314 N. Morris Street. 410-226-5111. The home of Robert Morris, signer of the Declaration of Independence was built in 1710. He was known as the "Financier of the American Revolution".
The 1876 B&B. 110 N. Morris Street. Oxford. 410-226-5496. Built 1876
Oxford Inn and Pope's Treasure. 504 S. Morris Street. 410-226-5220. Built by F.A. Delahaney Overery as an inn at turn of the century.
Combsberry. 4837 Evergreen Street. 410-226-5353. Built 1730. Elegant English country home on Brigham's Cove.
Nichols House. 217 S. Morris Street. 410-226-5799

Robert Morris Inn

Dining:

Robert Morris Inn. 314 N. Morris Street. 410-226-5111
Mill Street Grill. 101 Mill Street. 410-226-0400
Latitude 38. 26342 Oxford Road. 410-226-5303
Pier Street Marina and Restaurant.104 W. Pier Street. 410-226-5171
Schooner's Landing. Foot of Tilghman Street. 410-226-0160
Oxford Market and Deli. 203 S. Morris Street. 410-226-0015

Theater:

Tred Avon Players. Oxford Community Center

Trappe Station

Trappe Station was formerly a railroad shipping stop.

Jena. MD Rte. 333. This private home was built sometime after 1700. Jacob Gibson named it for one of Napoleon's victories. Mr. Gibson named other properties after other battles, including Friedland, Austerlitz and Marengo. During the War of 1812 he also owned Sharp's Island.

Trappe

Tucked away from Rte. 50 between Easton and Cambridge is the charming village of Trappe with many historic homes. Remains of a Trappist monastery still exist.

In 1883 17 year old Charles Kemp and 16 year old Percy Mullikin established the *Trappe Enterprise*, a weekly newspaper. The newspaper was printed until 1885. At that time Trappe had over 400 people, a grist mill and twenty seven businesses. Ferry boats called on the town and took passengers to Baltimore, Tolchester and other places on the Bay.

Baseball was a popular sport on the Eastern Shore and Trappe. J. Franklin "Home Run" Baker (1886-1963) was inducted into the Baseball Hall of Fame in 1955.

The first phone was installed in 1906.

Attractions:

Baker birthplace. J. Franklin "Home Run" Baker was born in Trappe in 1886. He played third base for the Philadelphia Athletics, and won two games with home runs during the 1911 World Series against the New York Giants. The house dates c1850.

Dickinson House. Maple Street. This was the family home of John Dickinson. John Dickinson was born at Crosiadore, which burned in 1976.

Compton. Private. Compton was patented to James Elvard in 1664 and was named in honor of Antonio LeCompte, an English cavalier who was the assignor of the original property. This home was acquired by William Stevens, a prominent Quaker, before 1679 and remained in the Stevens family to 1860. His great grandson John Stevens, who was expelled from the Quakers, inherited the house. His grandson Samuel Stevens, Jr. served as governor of Maryland (1822-25). The property has formal gardens, an allee of old maple trees, and a boxwood parterre.

Crosiadore. This was originally patented as "Croisdower" in 1667, "Crois Dower Marsh", and in 1695 "Crosedore Addition". John Dickinson was born here in 1732. He was the author of the 1768 "Letters from a Farmer in Pennsylvania to the Inhabitants of the British Colonies". Dickinson College, Carlise, Pennsylvania and Dickinson Bay off Howell Point Road were named for Mr. Dickinson. The plaque on Rte. 50 states that "Crosiadore" was still in the Dickinson family in 1939".

Jamaica Point. William R. Hughlett, a shipbuilder and director of Easton National Bank. built this late Federal-style house in 1838.

Hampden. This early 18th c house is an L-shaped house five bays long with a three bay brick kitchen attached. It is a fine example of early Talbot County architecture.

Lloyd's Landing. Private. This house was built by James Lloyd for his son James "the Mariner" c1720 who had a warehouse and wharf on the Choptank River.

Gibson Wright Mill House. This c1750 house is believed to have been built by Samuel Abbott, a miller. The house was sold to Gibson Wright in 1837.

Saulsbury. The land was bought by Peter Sharp in 1704 and house constructed c 1705. The original patent may date back to the 1660s.

Reed's Creek Farm. The land was patented to Thomas Reed in 1659. Later Nicholas Holmes bought the tract. His family sold this in 1765 to William Chaplain who built the house sometime before his death in 1813.

Belmont Farm. Private. Belmont was also built by William Hughlett of Easton c 1845.

Cherry Grove. Private. The c1860 house overlooking the Choptank River was owned by William Hughlett.

Chancellor's Point. This tract was given to Philip Calvert, brother of Cecil Calvert, the second Lord Baltimore. William Hughlett built the present house.

Ingleside. Private. The children of William Hughlett built this home in the 1840's.

Chlora's Point Farm. Private. This was part of the original "Heir Deir Lloyd tract" grant. Wings were added to the original structure in 1800, 1830, 1875 and 1920.

Walnut Grove. Private. The 1659 land grant has a house over 200 years old on the property. The graveyard has stones dating from 1794 to 1912.

The Wilderness. Private. The house is famous for its ghost "The Kissing Phantom of Trappe", a legend now over 100 years old. The lower wing of the house was built c1700 and was later owned by Daniel Martin, Governor of Maryland between 1829-31.

Scott's United Methodist Church. Religious services have been held on the property for over three hundred years, beginning with a Freinds Meeting House. Later it was home to the African Methodist Church, and became Scott's Church in 1869. The present building dates from 1880.

East New Market

East New Market was settled in 1660 on the North-South Choptank Indian trail as a village and site of a fort. The region was first mentioned in a grant to Henry Sewell in 1649 in London. The first white settler was thought to be John Edmonston who came from Virginia in the 1660's to seek religious freedom. Col. James O'Sullivane and two of the O'Sullivane brothers later joined him. The original name of the town was "Crossroads".

The New Market Academy was founded in 1818. The town was incorporated in 1884. The first mayor was Dr. George P. Jones. The Cambridge and Seaford Railroad began passing though here in 1868 and the Eastern Shore Railroad in 1898,

East New Market has been an agricultural center for three centuries. As horse racing became popular in 18thc Maryland, one of the tracks was located in New Market. In 1975 it became an Historic District and was entered in the National Register of Historic Places. Churches stand at the four entrances in to the town. A self-guided walking tour brochure is available.

Attractions:

Friendship Hall. This lovely private home was built in c 1740s and was home of Col. James O'Sullivane, quartermaster general of Dorchester County during the Revolution.

Buckland. This saltbox home was built for Dr. Daniel O'Sullivane and was once known as Maurice Hall.

Edmonston House. C 1780-90 and probably owned by O'Sullivane family. The Edmonston family bought the property known as "Liberty Hall" in 1840.

Little Manning House. C 18th c. This is located on property originally part of the Nanticoke Manor Tract c 1600.

Smith Cottage. This frame cottage was built c1760 probably by the O'Sullivane family.

House of the Hinges. c 1750 built by the Ennalls family. Lovely Federal home. It was later owned by Major Anthony Manning, a member of the Maryland Cavalry during the War of 1812, and later by his son, Dr. Anthony Manning, a Union surgeon during the Civil War. The name comes from the log building located behind the house, which has large hinges on the doors. In the 1920s it became the East New Market Hotel.

New Market House. c1780. The town was named for the house which sat on a tract of 7 seven acres. James O'Sullivane sold the property in 1787 to James Daffin, and it was sold again in 1790 to George Goodwin.

Dining:

Mike's Tavern. Main Street. 410-943-1207

Secretary

Secretary on Secretary Creek was founded in 1661 and incorporated in 1900. The creek was named for Henry Sewall, Secretary of the Province of Maryland in 1661.

Cartegena or My Lady Sewall's House. Willow Street. Private home. This house belonged to Henry Sewall, Secretary of Maryland under Gov. Charles Calvert, in 1661. Mrs. Sewall married Charles Calvert, later the third Lord Baltimore, after her husband's death. The paneling from the house is now at the Brooklyn Museum of Art.

Indian Purchase. MD Rte. 14. This was known as Goose Creek Farm. The land was originally a tract reserved for the Choptank Indians. Chief Hatchwop signed the deed transferring the land to Francis Taylor in 1693.

Dining:

Suicide Bridge Restaurant. 6304 Suicide Bridge Road. 410-943-4689. The restaurant offers cruises on board the paddle wheeler, Dorothy Megan.

Choptank

Boats used to sail three times daily between here (once called Medford's Wharf) and Baltimore.

Dover Bridge

Dover was a port during the 18th on the Choptank River. The bridge was built in 1869. In 1778 the General Assembly authorized the construction of a court house and prison, but the General Court continued to use the court house at Talbottown (now Easton).

Attractions:

Troth's Fortune. About a mile north of Dover Bridge is Troth's Fortune, built between 1686-1710. In 1676 William Troth patented two parcels of land – 400 acres of Troth's Fortune and 100 acres of Troth's Addition. In 1686 William

Troth I bought a 300 acre tract called Acton from John Acton. He became very well to do and active as a Quaker, even though he owned thirteen slaves. When William Troth died in 1710 he owned 1,216 acres in Talbot County, 500 in Dorchester County and over 240 acres in Queen Anne's County.

Hurlock

A railroad station was built here in 1867 for the Dorchester-Delaware Railroad. John Martin Hurlock opened the first grocery store at the railroad crossing in 1869. The town was incorporated in 1892.

Attractions:

The Old Train Station. The station has been restored and is available for excursions.

Hurlock Free Library. The library was established in 1900 and is the oldest public library on the Eastern Shore.

Lodging:

NorthFork B&B. 6505 Palmers Mill. 410-943-4706

Brookview

Brookview is the smallest municipality in the State of Maryland.

Attractions:

Marshyhope Wildlife Heritage Area. located on Marshyhope Creek, the principal tributary of the Nanticoke River.

Harmony

Attractions:

Col. Richardson Tomb and House Site. Colonel Richardson was an officer in the Revolutionary War and judge.

Dining:

Mary's Country Store. 6244 Harmony Road. 410-673-7263

Bethlehem

Dining:

Chance's Country Store. 21062 Dover Bridge Road. 410-673-7630

Federalsburg

This town was once known as Northwest Fork due to its location on the Nanticoke River. Cloudsberry Jones opened the first general store in 1789. Shipbuilding became the mainstay, using local white oak for shallow-draft river vessels. Iron furnaces, flour mills, sawmills and wood-carding mills also allowed the town to thrive. The Douglass iron furnace c1772 supplied materials for the Revolutionary War. Sawmills provided lumber to rebuild the U.S. Capitol and White House after they were burned during the War of 1812. Canning fruits also became an important industry. Messenger Mills, one of the largest flour mills on the Eastern Shore, operated at the turn of the 20th c.

Attractions:

Colonel Richardson High School. The school was named for William Richardson, an officer in the Revolutionary War and state district court judge.

Lodging:

Sandy Hill, A Country Inn. 324 S. Main Street. 410-754-5403. Historic building. has fireplaces in each room.
Idylwild Farm. 410-754-9141. This rustic inn is located on a farm.

Dining:

King's Buffet. 3350 Hayman Drive. 410-754-0888
Lane's Diner. 110 S. Main Street. 410-754-0001
Great Wall Chinese Restaurant. 119 S. Main Street. 410-754-8806
Recchioni's Soul of Italy. 111 S. Main Street. 410-754-0554
The New Village Inn. 402 Old Denton road. 410-754-2482
The Northwest Fork. 104 E. Central Avenue. 410-754-5745

Lincester

Lincester is one of the oldest settlements in Caroline County, and was known as Murray's Mill. The first gristmill operated here in 1681.

Preston

The town was founded around Frazier's Chapel in 1846. Preston became a railroad town after the Civil War. The town was first called Snow Hill, but later named for Alexander Preston, a Baltimore lawyer in 1856. During the 1940s and 50s three Underground Railroad stations operated in Preston. One of the stations was operated by Benjamin and Harriet Ross, parents of Harriet Tubman. Preston was chartered as a town in 1892. The Preston trucking line that had been around for many years shut down its operation in 1999.

Attractions:

Bethesda Methodist Church. Rte. 16 and 331. The church is on the site of one of the oldest Methodist churches in the United States, Frazier's Chapel and later called Bethesda Chapel in 1849. The chapel was built in 1785 by Rev. Freeborn Garrettson and Capt. William Frazier. The present church was built in 1875 and rebuilt in 1958.

Charles Dickerson Marker. Rte. 16, three miles north of Preston. Charles Dickerson was born on Wiltshire Manor in 1780 and moved to Foxley Hall in Easton in 1795. He was a lawyer and met Andrew Jackson when he was traveling to the U.S. Congress. He moved to Nashville, Tennessee and was killed by Jackson in a duel on May 30, 1806. His servant Truxton returned the body to Preston.

Linchester. Rte. 331. Hunting Creek Grist Mill was established here prior to 1681. Later Murray's Mill served farmers during the Revolutionary War. Linchester also served as a colonial port of entry. Caroline County Commissioners and the Caroline County historical Society have bought the property which they plan to restore.

Dining:

Pam's Place. Main Street. 410-673-7333

Cambridge

Cambridge was sighted by Captain John Smith on his trip up the Bay in 1608. The first settlers came in the mid 1600s. Cambridge was founded in 1684 as a port of entry by the General Assembly and incorporated in 1794. The town is located on the Choptank River, once part of the Choptank Indian Reservation. The name Cambridge was first used in 1686. The county courthouse was moved from Hardwood's Choice to Cambridge in 1687. In 1692 the Great Choptank Parish was one of the 30 officially established in Maryland. Cambridge is the county seat for Dorchester County.

This is the only deepwater port on the Eastern Shore. During the Revolutionary War Cambridge was the center for military operations on the Eastern Shore. During the mid 1800s large lumber and flour mills were located on Cambridge Creek. From here tobacco, muskrat pelts, and other products of the area, especially oysters during the 19th c were shipped. Timber was supplied to the Central Pacific Railroad for building rail cars. Later shipbuilding became prominent, mainly for the Chesapeake Bay trade.

In the late 1800s Col. James Wallace began packing oysters, and Cambridge was second to Baltimore in the number of oysters shucked per year. The refrigerated rail car improved transport of oysters, In 1911 Wallace's processing plant was sold to the Phillips Packing Company. The company left the area in the 1950's. The largest packer closed in 1961 and many people were left without jobs.

In 1910 a fire swept through Race and Muir Streets, burning a number of the buildings. Other fires took place downtown in 1882 and 1892.

In 1963 and 1967 the town had serious racial problems, and the Pine Street Elementary School was burned. In 1963 Gov. J. Millard Tawes had to send in the National Guard. H. Rap Brown prompted the 1967 incident. Once again the National Guard was called in by Gov. Spiro Agnew.

Cambridge has many lovely homes and a number of historic buildings. There are still shipyards along Cambridge Creek. The site of Yacht Maintenance was formerly the Cambridge Shipyard which built crash boats for the U.S. Navy during World War II. Take a cruise aboard the *Cambridge Lady* to see this lovely shoreline and some of the Choptank River.

Attractions

Christ Episcopal Church. High Street. The church was founded in 1693. The present building dates from 1883. Five governors of Maryland are buried here – John Henry, Charles Goldsborough, Henry Lloyd, Phillips Lee Goldsborough, and Emerson C. Harrington. Over the altar is a Tiffany stained glass window depicting Mary Magdalen washing Jesus' feet.

Dorcester County Historical Society.
Meredith House and Neild Museum. 902 LaGrange Avenue. 410-228-7953. The Meredith House is a Georgian home built c1760. The house has a collection of dolls and toys, and items from the seven Maryland governors who resided in Dorchester County. The Neild House has an herb garden, smokehouse, Indian and agricultural artifacts. On the grounds is the Governor Charles Goldsborough Stable dating from c1790.

Appleby. East Appleby Avenue. This was the home of Gov. Thomas H. Hicks. The house was built in the Georgian style and remodeled by Gov. Hicks into a Greek Revival home.

Long Wharf. The fountain, erected in 1918, is a memorial to those who gave their lives in World War I. The Franklin d. Roosevelt memorial was added in 1954.

Annie Oakley lived in Cambridge with her husband Frank Butler in a house built in 1912 at 28 Bellevue Avenue. She was a famous rifle woman and shot her first gun at age 9. Private home.

Harriet Tubman Museum & Educational Center. 424 Race Street. 410-228-0401. The museum traces Harriet Tubman's life from 1820-1913 and provides Underground Railroad tours.

Harriet Tubman Memorial Garden. Rte. 50 near Washington Street. The site was dedicated in 2000 and was created by the Maryland State Highway Administration to honor those who traveled to freedom along the Underground Railroad.

Many of the houses along High Street were built for members of the Goldsborough family. 200 High Street was built in 1790 for Charles Goldsborough. He became a US Congressman in 1805, and was the last Federalist Governor in Maryland, elected 1819. More than forty homes in Cambridge were built by J. Benjamin Brown, the first mayor of Cambridge.

100 High Street. Private home. Ellen S. Goldsborough, wife of Gov. Phillips Lee Goldsborough, built the house in 1903. A later owner was Gov. Emerson C. Harrington. Gov. Goldsborough was born at 111 High Street and lived at 102 High Street from 1912-16. His father M. Worthington Goldsborough lived at 106 High.

112 High Street. Private home. This was the home of William Vans Murray, a lawyer who served in the Maryland General Assembly and represented Congress from the Eastern Shore in 1791. He later was appointed minister to the Netherlands.

115 High Street. Joseph H. Johnson, a lawyer, member of the House of Delegate and senate built the house in 1882. He wrote the Maryland Oyster Laws. He also merged two newspapers to form the Democrat and News. He also built the Cambridge Marine Railway and Shipyard.

115 Mill Street. Private home. The house was built in 1923 by W. Grayson Winterbottom, a founder of the Phillips Packing Company.

312 Mill Street. Private home. The house was completed by Captain Levi Phillips, founder of Phillips Packing Company.Leon Craford designed the house

which was built on the site of the Zion Church which was located here from 1802-46 and known as Garrettsons Chapel..

Zion Methodist Church. 612 Locust Street. The church was built in 1911 in the Gothic Revival style.

701 Locust Street. Private home. The house was built for Judge Henry Lloyd who served as Governor of Maryland 1886-88.

Captain Harvey Conway House. Private. The Queen Anne Style house was built between 1896-1900 with a wraparound porch added in the 1920s. Captain Conway was once the owner of the largest sailing fleet on the Chesapeake Bay. He had an oyster dredging business and shipped pineapples from the West Indies. He also owned 80 houses in Cambridge.

Dorchester County Courthouse. 206 High Street. The building was built in 1854 and designed by Richard Upjohn, the architect of Trinity Church, New York. The courthouse was the site of a civil lawsuit in regards to the legal ownership of Harriet tubman's mother and children. Ms. Tubman also used the site to meet Keziah and John Bowley when she was being given her freedom from slavery. Several trials took place here regarding those who were helping the slaves. Reverend Samuel Green who helped Harriet Tubman and owned a copy of "Uncle Tom's Cabin" received a ten year jail sentence.

Bayly House. 207 High Street. This house was built in Annapolis in 1755 and moved across the Bay in 1760 by John Caille, an 18th c merchant. He leased 205 High Street from the Great Choptank Parish in 1750.

The Glenburn. Glenburn Avenue. This was originally part of the 800 acre Glasgow plantation. It was given to Benjamin B. Tubman by his father Dr. Robert Tubman c1842 as a wedding present. The three story house has a "widow's walk" between the two chimneys.

Ayrshire. Private home. Ayshire was also part of Glasgow and the Tubman family. The Georgian house was built in 1920 on the remaining 285 acres.

Sycamore Cottage. 417 High Street. Built after 1759 by Rev. Daniel Maynadier, a French Huguenot. Now home of the Cambridge Women's Club.

Waugh Methodist Episcopal Church. 429 High Street. A church has been on the site since 1826. the present church was built in 1901 to serve the black community. Half of the cost of the original organ was paid for by Andrew Carnegie.

Bethel A.M.E. Church. Bethel and Pine Streets. The church was built in 1870 and renovated in 1903. It houses the oldest A.M.E. congregation in Cambridge.

Grace Methodist Church. Race and Muir Streets. The Gothic Revival church was built c1881 and designed by Benjamin Brown.

Stanley Institute or Rock School. Rte. 16 and Bayley Road. 410-754-9091. By appointment. This is one of the oldest schools organized by the Black community in Maryland. C1867 the building was moved from Church Creek to the Christ Rock community. It has served both as a church and school. The present Rock Methodist Church was built in the 19th c. The institute is now a museum.

Piney Point on Phillips Creek. The plantation was purchased in 1690, and the house completed in 1710.

Horn Point. Two miles west of Cambridge is Horn Point, once part of the 600 acre plantation of John Horne in 1658. Horne transferred the property to Richard Preston of Calvert County, who was a burgess from 1653-1668. Charles Goldsborough later bought the property and by 1747 had enlarged the property to 1,020 acres. When he died in 1767 he owned over 10,000 acres.

In 1912 Thomas Coleman DuPont, an industrialist and U.S. Senator purchased the property and built a house. His son Francis P. DuPont built an air strip. He donated the site to the city of Cambridge. Renovations to the buildings took place and in 1975 an oyster hatchery opened. Today the Horn Point Lab strives to restore the Chesapeake Bay ecology with the addition of the $26 million Aquaculture and Restoration Ecology Laboratory, dedicated in 2003.

About six miles west of Cambridge on Rte. 343 is the Spocott Windmill, a reproduction of a "post mill". It was named for Spocott Plantation that was patented to Stephen Gary in 1662 on Gary Creek.

Brannock Maritime Museum. 210 Talbot Avenue. 410-228-1245. Great photographs and nautical artifacts from Dorchester County's maritime heritage.

Richardson Maritime Museum and Boatworks. 401 High Street. 410-228-1871. The museum is named for James Richardson, an Eastern Shore shipbuilder. His boat, *Mr. Jim*, can be seen at the Chesapeake Bay Museum at St. Michael's. He built a replica of *The Dove*, one of the original ships to sail to St. Mary's City. On display are Chesapeake Bay ship models.

In October 2004 the Richardson Museum and Brannock Museum announced that would build a new museum devoted to local maritime history on the property of the Boatworks on Cambridge Creek.

Dorchester Arts Center. 120 High Street. 410-228-7782. This building is located in an 1892 Victorian hotel. The center has changing art exhibits and classes.

Dorchester Heritage Museum. 1904 Horn Point Road. 410-228-1899. Just west of Cambridge is an old airplane hangar on a former duPont estate. The museum has a Watermen Room, Aviation Hall, Archeology and Heritage displays.

J.M. Clayton Company. The company was started as an oyster shucking business in the 1890s on a wooden island. It later became one of the first crabmeat processing plants in Dorchester County. J. Clayton Brooks developed the first commercial crab picking machine.

Nathan of Dorchester. Long Wharf. 410-228-7141. The boat is the last skipjack built on the Bay in 1994 for Harold Ruark who grew up on Cassons Neck just outside Cambridge. His grandfather had built skipjacks and she is modeled after the *Myrtle* and *Oriole*. She is used as a living museum and is dedicated to the wooden boat heritage of the Bay. Educational programs, camps and field trips are offered.

Cambridge Lady Cruises. Trenton Street Dock. 410-221-0776. Cruise boat

Cambridge Lady

Dorchester County Public Library. The building is located on the site of an 18th c mansion, the Hill, which was the home of John Woolford. He and his wife are buried in front of the library.

Cambridge Cemetery. Gov. Holiday Hicks is buried here. He blocked the Maryland General Assembly from passing legislation that would have brought Maryland into the Confederacy.

Academy School. 201 Mill Street. The school was built in c1900. The original school known as The Cambridge Academy was incorporated in 1812 and destroyed by fire in 1902.

Channel Charters. Municipal Yacht Basin. 410-228-1645. Cruise on board *Satisfaction.*

Tourist Information:

Sailwinds Park. Foot of Frederick C. Malkus, Jr. Bridge

Tours:

Harriet Tubman Museum & Educational Center. 424 Race Street. African American heritage tours
Brooks Barrel Company. Bucktown Road. The barrel company is the last remaining stack cooperage in Maryland. Barrels are made from native pine. Tours are by appointment.
Buckstown Heritage Tours. 4303 Bucktown Road. 410-901-9255
Cambridge Historic Tours. 410-228-5563
Ghost Walk on Historic High Street. Dorchester Arts Center. 410-228-7782

Lodging:

Hyatt Regency Chesapeake Bay Golf Resort, Spa and Marina. 2800 Ocean Gateway. 410-901-1234. Resort and golf course set on the Choptank River
Glasgow Inn. 1500 Hambrooks Boulevard. 410-228-0575. This is the ancestral home of the Tubman family. It was purchased by Dr. Robert F. Tubman in 1842. Originally on land purchased by Dr. William Murray Ward, a surgeon who had come from Scotland, in 1760 and built the house that year. He owned about one third of the property in Cambridge. His grandson, William Vans Murray was Minister to Holland in 1800, and negotiated the Louisiana Purchase with France. He also was elected to Congress.
Cambridge House**.** 112 High Street. 410-221-7700. Former captain's mansion
Lodgecliffe on the Choptank**.** 103 Choptank Terrace. 410-228-1760. Nice views of the Choptank River
Commodore's Cottage. 210 Talbot Avenue. 410-228-6938

Cambridge Inn. Rte. 50. 410-221-0800
Day's Inn & Suites. 2917 Ocean Gateway. 410-228-4444
Best Value Inn. 2831 Ocean Gateway. 410-221-0800
Quality Inn. 2335 Wingate-Bishop's Head Road. 410-338-6900
Holiday Inn Express. 2715 Ocean Gateway. 410-221-9900

Dining:

Canvasback Restaurant & Irish Pub. 420 Race Street. 410-221-7888
Water's Edge Grill. Hyatt Regency Chesapeake Bay. 100 Heron Blvd. 410-901-6400
Snapper's Waterfront Café. 112 Commerce Street. 410-228-0112.
Blue Point Provision Company. Hyatt Regency. 100 Heron Blvd. 410-901-1234
Cambridge Diner. 2924 Old Rte. 50. 410-228-8898
The Blue Crab Restaurant on the Water. 203 Trenton Street 410-228-8877
Kay's Country Kitchen. 2831 Ocean Highway. 410-901-8844
Ocean Odyssey Seafood Delicatessen. Rte. 50. 410-228-8633
Pizza Palace. 600 Sunburst Highway. 410-221-0022
Portside Seafood Restaurant. 201 Trenton Street. 410-228-9007
Place on Race Café. 421 Race Street. 410-228-0833
High Spot Restaurant. 303 High Street. 410-228-3410
McGuigan's Pub and Restaurant. 411 Muse Street. 410-228-7110
Spicer's Seafood. Rte. 50 and Woods Road. 410-221-0222
The Great American Diner. 2924 Old Rte. 50. 410-228-8898. Open 24 hours
Doris Mae's. 400 Race Street. 410-228-0866
Little Danny's Sugar Shack & Deli. 400 Academy Street. 410-221-7745
Simmons Center Market. 600 Race Street. 410-228-4313
Gale Winds Restaurant. 203 Trenton Street. 410-221-1086
Runway Café. 5227 Bucktown Road. 410-221-5080
Big Mario's Rustican Pizza Italian Restaurant. Dorchester Square. 410-228-1515
Great Wall Chinese Food. Sunburst Center. 410-228-0332
Peking House Restaurant. 2717 Ocean Gateway. 410-228-94242
Sandy's Restaurant. 400 Race Street. 410-228-0866
Sub City. 1721 Race Street. 410-228-8339
The Shoals. Rte. 50. 410-228-7599
Shirley's Restaurant. 1504 Glasgow Street. 410-228-2522
The Creek Deli. 106 Market Square. 410-228-1161
The Dog House Restaurant. 2839 Ocean Gateway. 410-221-5100
Dayton's. 1-A Sunburst Highway. 410-228-9873

Bucktown

Attractions:

Birthplace of Harriet Tubman. Greenbriar Road on the site of Bodress Plantation. Harriet Tubman (Araminta "Minty" Ross) was born a slave in 1820 and escaped to the north in 1849. She is called the "Moses" of her people. She organized the Underground Railroad freeing more than 300 slaves. She returned 19 times to Delmarva to free other slaves. During the Civil War she was in the Union Army as a nurse, scout and spy. Later she settled in Auburn, New York and was a founder of the Women's Suffrage Movement. She founded a home for needy and elderly African-Americans and died in 1913.

Bucktown Village Store. 4303 Bucktown Road. 410-901-9255. At this location Harriet tubman was struck by a two pound weight. She believed God gave her the insight to guide slaves to their freedom.

Bazzel Church. Bestpitch Ferry Road. Harriet Ross Tubman's family worshipped here in the 1800's. After the Civil War Mrs. Tubman became active in women's suffrage and temperance movements. She and others organized the African Methodist Episcopal Zion Church. A newer church has been built in front of the older one.

Cook Point

Just west of Cambridge is Cook Point. The point received its name from Andrew Cook, who was the father of Ebenezer Cook, deputy receiver-general to the fifth Lord Baltimore and the first poet laureate of Maryland. He came to Maryland from England about 1661. In 1662 he bought "Maulden" or "Cook's Point" in Dorchester County.

In 1659 Anthony LeCompte, a French Huguenot, was granted 800 acres at Castle Haven, on Cooke's Point opposite Choptank Island, which he called "Antonine".

Church Creek

Church Creek developed around Trinity Church built c1690. Land records date back to about 1700. The town was known to have a shipyard in 1766.

Attractions:

Old Trinity Church. 1716 Taylor's Island Road. 410-228-2940. This is the oldest Episcopal Church in the Maryland still in use and built c1675. The church is very small, only twenty feet by thirty-eight feet. The church sits on an 85 Glebe on Church Creek. The church was established in 1692 as Dorchester Parish and until 1853 was known as Dorchester Parish Church. The floor tiles are laid on a bed of burnt oysters. The pulpit is three-tiered. Queen Anne gave the communion chalice. Col. Edgar Garbish restored the church in 1956 as a memorial to his father-in-law Walter P. Chrysler, founder of the Chrysler Corporation. Gov. Thomas King Carroll and his daughter Anna Ella Carroll are buried in the graveyard. Anna Ella Carroll was a silent member of President Lincoln's Cabinet.

Gibson House. Daniel T. Owen, an abolitionist and delegate to the Republican convention that nominated Abraham Lincoln built this house just after the Civil War.

Wyvill House. Just west of Church Creek on Rte. 16. Dr. Dorsey Wyvill was one of the founders of the Medical and Chirurigical (surgeon) Faculty of Maryland in 1799.

Giant Mosquito sculpture. Rte. 16

Lodging:

Loblolly Landings & Lodge. 2142 Liners Road. 410-397-3033. Lodge with fishing pond, airstrip, bike and canoe rentals, hiking trails.

Fishing Creek

Dining:

Old Salty's Restaurant. 2560 Hoopers Island Road. 410-397-3752

Woolford

Woolford was originally named Milton and then Loomtown for its many weaver's looms. An Act of the Assembly in 1682 authorized the county court to pay 10 pounds of tobacco per yard of wool three-quarters yard wide. This was later repealed. The name comes from Samuel W. Woolford, postmaster in 1902.

Lodging:

Liberty Hall. 1608 Taylor's Island Road. 410-228-9780. The Inn at Woolford's Delight was established in 1817. Whitefield Woolford built Liberty Hall as a gift for his bride. The rooms are decorated with early antiques and include the Sir Charles Marston Room and Captain Josiah's Room. Josiah Bartlett was the second Signer of the Declaration of Independence.

Taylor's Island

Settlers planted crops here as early as 1659. Shipbuilding became an important industry, but ceased around 1850 when the lumber supply was depleted.

Attractions:

All of these buildings are in the National Register of historic Places.

Chapel of Ease, The chapel, known as Grace Church, has been part of Dorchester Parish since 1762. the present building was completed in 1873 in the "Country gothic" style.

Becky Phipp's Cannon. Ret. 16 after crossing the Taylor's Island Bridge. The cannon dates from the War of 1812. During an ice jam on the island the Taylor's Island militia seized the British warship *Dauntless*, taking 20 prisoners and this 12 pound cannon.

Dorchester Schoolhouse. The first schoolhouse in Dorchester County dates to c 1785

Bethlehem M.E. Church. The church dates back to 1787 and is the oldest Methodist Church in Dorchester County.

Ridgeton. This home was completed in 1857 for Judge Levi D. Travers.

Taylor's Island Museum. Off Rte. 16. 410-221-1207. By appointment. The museum is located in a 1916 schoolhouse. The exhibit includes Native American artifacts, a cobbler's shop, and items relating to the Bay.

Lodging:

Becky Phipps Inn. 638 Taylor's Island Road. 410-221-2911

Airey

The town was named for Thomas Airey who came from England in 1726 and became rector of Great Choptank Parish. In 1781 Freeborn Garrettson preached the first Methodist sermon in the United States at the home of Henry Airey. The village was moved north in the 1800s and became a station on the Cambridge and Seaford Railroad.

Blackwater National Wildlife Refuge

Blackwater National Wildlife Refuge is located off Route 16. This 23,000 acre refuge has tours, trails, biking, rare birds, animals, and marshes. Four rivers – the Blackwater, Little Blackwater, Transquaking, and Chicamacomico empty into Fishing Bay.

Attractions:

Applegarth House. MD 335 just after refuge. This farmhouse is on land received as a patent by Richard Tubman in 1670 for fighting the Indians. He was a Catholic settler from St. Mary's.

Golden Hill

Lodging:

Twin Willows Farm. Meekins Neck Road. 609-829-8354. This 1200 acre estate is located near Blackwater National Wildlife Refuge.
Chesapeake Retreats. 1-888-726-7662. Farm located just outside Cambridge

Wingate

Lodging:

Wingate Manor B&B. 2335 Wingate-Bishop's Head Road. 410-397-8717

Whitehaven

The village is part of a 1663 land grant that was called Noble Quarter. This was later divided into Ignoble Quarter and Might Have Had More. Whitehaven was chartered in 1685 and was an official Port of Entry. The town was noted as a port, for shipbuilding and during the 1920's, for rum running.

Whitehaven was established in 1700 by Col. George Hale who had come from Whitehaven, Cumberlandshire, England. He married Mildred Warner Washington, whom had been married to Lawrence Washington. Their son, Augustine Washington, was the father of George Washington.

The Whitehaven Ferry after 300 plus years, still provides continuous service across the Wicomico River. The ride is about three minutes. The entire village is on the National Historic Register.

Attractions:

Whitehaven Heritage Association. 2764 Whitehaven Road. 410-873-2939

Lodging:

Whitehaven Bed & Breakfast. 23844 River Street. 410-873-3294. The B&B occupies the Otis Lloyd House (c1850s) and the Charles Leatherbury House (c1886).
Whitehaven Hotel. 23844 River Street. 410-873-3294

Dining:

Red Roost Restaurant. 2670 Clara Road. 410-546-5443

Madison

Madison is on the Little Choptank River and dates to before 1760 when it was called Tobacco Stick. It was probably named for President James Madison. Emerson C. Harrington, Governor of Maryland was born here in 1864.

Hodson House. Rte.16. Only the site remains of this house owned by John Hodson, an early justice. The house once served as the Dorchester County Court House.

Dining:

Madison Bay Sea & Sea. Madison Canning Road. 410-228-4111. Restaurant, marina and campground

Hoopers Island

Hoopers Island was settled by the Hoopers, a Catholic family in the 17th c. Three islands - Upper, Middle and Lower Hooper, make up the area that is separated from the mainland by the Honga River. Some of the earliest land grants in Dorchester County were issued here in 1659. The islanders were originally farmers, but most now make their livelihood from the Bay.

Attractions:

St. Mary's Star of the Sea Church. This Catholic Church was erected in 1872. Nearby is the site of the first Catholic Church built in Dorchester County, probably by Richard Tubman.

Plymouth. Now a county park, this site was used to grow tobacco beginning in 1707. In 1748 the Assembly ordered a public tobacco warehouse be built at Plymouth Town. In 1773 this was sold. During the Revolutionary War a militia company called the Plymouth Greens was formed.

Lakesville

Capt. Henry Lake fought in the Revolutionary War. His daughter Lavinia became a heroine by fighting off Tory picaroons (pirates) who tried to steal the silver buckles off her shoes. While she was locked in a room the picaroons set fire to the house. Lavinia escaped and put out the blaze. She then found her father's militia who chased the men away. Capt. Lake became High Sheriff in 1797.

Linkwood and Salem

These agricultural communities date back to the 1600's. They are centered around a native American trail and chapel.

Vienna

Vienna is one of the oldest settlements on the Eastern Shore, dating back to 1669, and was once called Emperors Landing, or the "Town on the Nanticoke", as it is located on the Nanticoke River. 100 acres of the town are from a patent Lord Baltimore received, part of 6,000 acres in Dorchester County. The Colonial Assembly recommended the point as a ferry location in 1671.

Vienna was founded by a decree of the Colonial Assembly in 1706. Jacob Lockerman was appointed to lay out the town. He suggested naming it for Vienna, Austria. It may also have been named for Vinnacokasimmon, an Indian chief. In 1768 the town became the Custom's District for the region, and the original Custom's House still stands. Shipbuilding and cotton were important trades.

During the American Revolutionary War goods and supplies were shipped from here to the Continental Army, and it was raided by the British five times. During the War of 1812 the British came up the Nanticoke River. Thomas Holiday

Hicks, governor of Maryland at the time of the Civil War lived here from 1829-40.

The Delmarva Power and Light Company has a large facility on the western side of the bridge over the Nanticoke River. A bridge first crossed the Nanticoke in 1828, was rebuilt in 1931 and the present bridge dates from 1989. The river forms the boundary between Dorchester and Wicomico counties.

Attractions:

Vienna Heritage Museum. 303 Race Street. 410-376-3620. The museum displays aspects of rural life and industry in Vienna. Exhibits include equipment from the last Mother of Pearl factory in the United States.

Governor Thomas Holiday Hicks House. Water Street. Home of the governor who prevented Maryland from seceding during Civil War.

The Customs House. Church and Water Streets. This building dates from 1768.

Nanticoke Reservation. Indiantown Road. Vinnacokasimmon or Unnacokassimon was Emperor to the Nanticoke Indians about 1677 at Chicacone. This Indian reservation was established in 1698 by an act of Assembly along the Nanticoke River. The white settlers and Indians often clashed and the Indians had to petition the General Assembly a number of times for aid. The reservation was 5166 ¼ acres. Most of the tribe left for other states and Canada, and all were gone by 1800.

St. Paul's Episcopal Church was founded in 1709.

Lodging:

Tavern House B&B. 111 Water Street. 410-376-3347. C1800. The building is a restored colonial tavern and overlooks the river.
Nanticoke Manor House. Church Street. 410-376-3432. This also overlooks the river. Captain James Kendall Lewis bought the house in 1861 and added the three story brick onto the 18th rear frame. He owned an extensive sailing fleet and was also a farmer. He smuggled goods to the Confederacy during the Civil war. The house is supposed to have several ghosts.
Governor's Ordinary. Water & Church Streets
Florida Point Farms. 4710 Ravenwood Road. 410-376-0342

Dining:

Nanticoke Inn. Church Street. 410-376-3432

Elliott Island

Elliott Island is about 18 miles south of Vienna, located on Fishing Bay. If you drive down Elliott Island road you can see ancient salt marshes. The town once had a population of 600, but only about 70 now.

Mardela Springs.

Mardela Springs was formerly the village of Barren Creek. A spring has been here since Indian times. In the 1800s it became a health resort. The General Assembly changed the name in 1906 to Mardela Springs combining the names of Maryland and Delaware. The springs are in a brick springhouse.

Attractions:

Adkins Historical and Museum Complex, Inc. Brattan Street. 410-749-4871. This was created by J. Howard and Louise Adkins over a period of fifteen years. On the property are the:

- Brattan-Taylor village store, with ledgers dating from 1848-77
- Odd Fellows Lodge Hall, originally the carpenter shop of Thomas J. Windsor
- Livery stable c 1905
- The Gravenor-English one room schoolhouse that was built and deeded to Somerset County by Thomas Gravenor
- The Young Purchase Farmhouse, built by William Young c1724 and used continuously until the 1960s. Behind this are the gravestone of a Revolutionary War Patriot and his wife who were the ancestors of Orville and Wilbur Wright.
- The Contractors shed built in the 1950s to resemble the office of Dr. Lemuel R. Brattan
- Another Contractors shed honoring those who served in the military
- The warehouse for local cannery that operated from 1903 to 1936

Mason-Dixon Middlestone. MD Rte. 54. This marks the mid-point of the line surveyed in 1750-51 from Fenwick Island on the Delaware Bay to the Chesapeake Bay which established the Delaware-Maryland boundary. It was named for Charles Mason and Jeremiah Dixon who finished the survey in 1763. To the south was Calvert land, and to the North Penn. The marker was erected in 1768.

Sharptown

The town was settled in 1769 on the Nanticoke River.

Quantico

Quantico dates from the 18th c and several homes remain from that period. The town is listed as historic district.

Delmar

Delmar was originally built at the end of a railroad line. The Mason-Dixon marker is 6.5 miles west of here.

Lodging:

Delmarva Inn & Conference Center. 9544 Ocean Highway. 410-896-3434
Traveler Motel. 9461 Ocean Highway. 410-742-8701

Dining:

Old Mill Crab House & Restaurant. Rte. 54 & Waller Road. 302-846-2808

Reliance

Attractions:

Patty Cannon's house. Private. Once a tavern, it was also known to house kidnappers, bank robbers, and murderers.

Eldorado

Attractions:

Rehobeth. Rte. 14. The area was patented in 1673 to John Lee, son of Col. Richard Lee, and the founder of the Lee family in Virginia. The house was built c1725.

Pukkum. this small community's motto is "You can't get there from here."

Hebron

Hebron dates back to the 1890s and was a railroad village.

Attractions:

St. Paul's Episcopal Church. Rte. 50. The church as established in 1711-1725 as a Chapel of Ease for Green Hill Church which was established in 1694. This simple, but elegant white clabbered church was built in 1773.

St. Paul's Church

Chesapeake Fire Museum. Rte. 670. 410-860-0843. Has a fine example of fire equipment.

Springhill Church. Just north of Hebron on Rte. 347. This church was built in 1771-72 as an Anglican Chapel.

Dining:

Hebron Family Restaurant. 201 S. Main Street. 410-749-9955

Green Hill

Attractions:

Green Hill Episcopal Church. Green Hill Church Road. This church was built on the Wicomico River in 1733 and has the oldest graveyard in U.S. Open by appointment.

Tyaskin

Dining:

Boonie's. 21438 Nanticoke Road. 410-548-7879

Bivalve

The town is named for the many crustaceans found here. The Great North American Turtle Races take place here.

Nanticoke

Nanticoke is named for the Indian tribe that inhabited the area. The town was founded c1809 on Nanticoke Point. The oyster industry was very important in the late 1800s and an oyster fleet is still located here.

Bloodsworth Island

Bloodsworth Island is located near Deal. The island has been used by the Navy for target practice since 1942. In 1997 nesting osprey forced the cancellation of this practice. The name comes from the Bloodsworth family.

Deal Island

The island was first called Devil's Island by the survivors of a 17th c shipwreck. People pronounced this as Dea'vil Island, which eventually was shortened to Deal Island. It was later home to Joshua Thomas, "Parson of the Islands" who established many Methodist churches in the area. He traveled in a log canoe named *The Methodist*. The island has three Methodist Churches where the sarcophagi are above ground due to the marshy area.

Crabbing and oystering are very important, and Deal is said to have the largest number of skipjacks still around.

Almodington. MD 363. John Elzey received a patent in 1661 and served as a Maryland commissioner to govern the Manokin and Annemessex settlements. His son, Arnold Elzey built Almodington. Unfortunately it burned in 1993. The woodwork from the dining room and a mantle were salvaged and are at the Metropolitan Museum of Art in New York City.

Deal Island Wildlife Management Area. MD Rte. 363 10,000 acre refuge.

Joshua Thomas Chapel and Grave. 1776-1853

Shopping:

Arby's General Store. Main Street. Wenona. Our favorite sign reads " It ain't the end of the world, but you can see it from here!"
Arby and Deb's Sea Rations. Deal Island. 410-784-2313

Salisbury

James Rhodeson acquired 200 acres on the river in 1667 and named the town for Salisbury, England. Salisbury was laid out in 1732 on 20 lots around Handy's Landing, set up by Col. Issac Handy in c1665. It was incorporated in 1811. The town is located on the Wicomico River and is the largest city on the Eastern Shore. During the Revolutionary War the city asked the Continental Congress for assistance in staving off British predators. William Smallwood led a small militia in this effort. Alexander Roxburgh, a Scot, served with Gen. Smallwood. He was promoted to captain after the Battle of Long Island, and later became a major. Mr. Roxburgh eloped with Frances Handy, daughter of Col. Isaac Handy of Pemberton Hall.

In 1852 the steamboat *Wilson Smart* began running between Baltimore and Salisbury. At about the same time the Philadelphia, Wilmington and Baltimore Railroad reached Salisbury. The Wicomico and Pocomoke Railroad linked

Salisbury in 1868. Refrigerated freight service began in 1901, and Salisbury was to become a commercial shipping hub. A number of sawmills brought fortunes to several families. William Jackson owned property on the Eastern Shore and 140,000 acres of land in Alabama. Elihu Jackson, whose family made their wealth through the lumber business, became governor of Maryland in 1887.

Salisbury is the location of the Perdue Chicken headquarters. US Senator Paul Sarbanes was born in Salisbury, and actor John Glover grew up here. The National Indoor Tennis Championships were once held at the Civic Center which later burned down.

Some of the city was destroyed by fires in 1869 and 1886. The first African American high school on the Eastern Shore was established here in 1919.

Today Salisbury is home to the Ward Museum of Waterfowl Art, the Salisbury Zoo and a number of historic buildings. The downtown Plaza has restaurants and shops or you can walk along the river.

Attractions:

Ward Museum of Waterfowl Art. 909 S.Schumaker Drive. 410-742-4988. The wonderful collection of decoys includes master carvers Lemuel and Steven Ward and other carvers and painters.

Poplar Hill Mansion. 117 Elizabeth Street. 410-749-1776. Built 1795 by Major Levin Handy, an officer in the Revolution.

New Nithsdale. Pemberton Drive. This private home was built by Capt. Levin Gale, a merchant and planter c1735. The name came from Mr. Gale's daughter's husband, Capt. William Murray, a sea captain, who named it for his Scottish hometown.

Mason-Dixon Line Marker. MD Rte. 467. Has coat of arms of George Washington and Lord Baltimore

The Salisbury Times is on the site of Camp Upton, a Civil War camp.

Ellis Bay Wildlife Management Area. 1,924 preserve.

Salisbury Zoological Park. 750 South Park Drive.410-548-3188

Rockawalkin School. Pemberton Drive. The one-room schoolhouse was built 1872.

Salisbury State University. Salisbury Boulevard. The General Assembly established a teacher's college for the Eastern Shore in 1922. This opened as the State Normal School in Salisbury in 1925. It was renamed the State Teachers College at Salisbury in 1935, Salisbury State College in 1963, and Salisbury State University in 1988.

Salisbury State University

Edward H. Nabb Research Center. 1101 Camden Avenue. 410-543-6312. For those interested in genealogical information please visit the center on the University campus.

Atrium Gallery. Salisbury State University. 410-543-6271

Fulton Hall Gallery. Salisbury State University. 410-543-6270

Salisbury State University Arboretum. 1101 Camden Avenue. 410-543-6323.Tthe arboretum has lovely gardens, a sculpture park, and greenhouse.

Pemberton Hall and Park. Pemberton Drive. 410-742-1741. This was built in 1741 for Col. Isaac Handy. He had a fleet of ships and was one of the founders of Salisbury. Capt. Allison Parsons, a Confederate, occupied the house during the Civil War.

Chipman Cultural Center. 321 Broad Street. 410-860-9290. The building is used for various town cultural functions. It was originally the John Wesley A.M.E Church, the oldest African-American church on the Eastern Shore. The land was purchased by 5 African-American freedmen in 1837 and part of the church built in 1838. In 1876 it was incorporated as the John Wesley Methodist Episcopal Church. Mr. and Mrs. Charles P. Chipman purchased the building, and gave the building to the Chipman Foundation. Mr. Chipman was Principal of the Colored Industrial High School, and later Salisbury High School.

Salisbury Art Institute and Gallery, Inc. 212 W. Main Street. 410-546-9971

Delmarva Research Center for History and Culture. Power and Wayne Streets. 410-543-6312

Eastern Shore Baseball Hall of Fame. 6400 Hobbs Road. 410-546-4444

Excel Interactive Science Museum. 210 W. Main Street. 410-546-2168

Wicomico Heritage Center. Pemberton Drive. 410-860-0447

Lodging:

Ramada Inn & Conference Center. 300 S. Salisbury Blvd. 410-546-4400
Days Inn Salisbury. 2525 North Salisbury Boulevard. 410-749-6200
Comfort Inn. 2701 N. Salisbury Blvd. 410-543-4666
Best Budget Inn. 1804 N. Salisbury Blvd. 410-546-2238
Best Western Salisbury Plaza. 1735 N. Salisbury Blvd. 410-546-1300
Best Value Inn. 2625 N. Salisbury Blvd. 410-742-7194
Economy Inn. 1500 N. Salisbury Blvd. 410-749-6178
Hampton Inn. 121 E. Naylor Mill Road. 410-334-3080
Lord Salisbury Inn. 2637 N. Salisbury Blvd. 410-742-3251
Microtel Inn & Suites. 3050 Merritt Mill Road. 410-742-2626
Sleep Inn. 406 Punkin Ct.. 410-572-5516

Super 8 Motel. 2615 N. Salisbury Blvd. 410-749-5131
Temple Hill Motel. 1510 S. Salisbury Blvd. 410-742-3284
Thrift Travel Inn. 603 N. Salisbury Blvd. 410-742-5135

Restaurants:

Brew River Restaurant. 502 W. Main Street. 410-677-6757
Chesapeake Steakhouse. 1801 N. Salisbury Blvd. 410-742-8000
Chili's Grill and Bar. 2750 N. Salisbury Blvd. 410-860-4700
DiPietor's N.Y. Pizzeria. 211 Milford Street. 410-543-1911
English Company. 604 S. Schumaker Drive. 410-742-9511
Fuji Sushi Bar. 1014F Salisbury Blvd. 410-219-5608
Golden Star Diner. 507 W. Salisbury Pkwy. 410-219-5150
Island Way. 2065 N. Salisbury Blvd. 410-341-3636
Jumbo Buffet. 917 S. Salisbury Blvd. 410-749-9188
Sage Diner. 917 S. Salisbury Blvd. 410-860-9158
Pestos Bar & Grill. 401 Snow Hill Road. 410-548-1058
Flannery's. 327 E. Main Street. 410-546-2570
Market Street Inn. 130 W. Market Street. 410-742-4145
Watermen's Cove. 925 Snow Hill Road. 410-546-1400
Cactus Taverna. 2420 N. Salisbury Blvd. 410-548-1254
Greek Pita Place. 800 S. Salisbury Blvd. 410-543-8600
Fratelli's Restaurant. 1306 S. Salisbury Blvd. 410-341-0807
Chesapeake Bagel Bakery. 1006 S. Salisbury Blvd. 410-543-8249
Hunan Delight. 901 N. Salisbury Blvd. 410-860-0111
HuNan Palace. Accurate Suburban Center. 410-546-5990
Imperial Gallery. 315 Civic Avenue. 410-546-3103
LaRoma. 934 S. Salisbury Blvd. 410-742-2380
LaTolteca Mexican Restaurant. 110 Truitt Street. 410-749-8663
Emperor's Kitchen. 1147 S. Salisbury Blvd. 410-749-6336
Dayton's Restaurant. 909 Snow Hill Road. 410-548-2272
East Side Delicatessen. 1120 E. Main Street. 410-543-2656
Subside Deli. 106 Truitt Street. 410-742-0094
Goin Nuts Café. 947 Mt. Hermon Road. 410-860-1164
Zia's Pastaria. 2408 N. Salisbury Blvd. 410-543-9118
Ponzetti's Pizza & Subs. 1053 N. Salisbury Blvd. 410-546-1251
Break Time. 1009 S. Salisbury Blvd. 410-742-7665
Café Milano. 901 N. Salisbury Blvd. 410-749-4100
China Express. 1125 New Bedford Way. 410-742-2800
Chinatown Buffet. 2722 N. Salisbury Blvd. 410-860-6886
Deli Master. 215 North Blvd. 410-742-3354
DeVage's Italian Subs. 119 W. College Avenue. 410-334-2200
Downtown Deli. 212 W. Main Street. 410-749-0611
English's North. N. Salisbury Blvd. 410-742-8183
English's South. 735 S. Salisbury Blvd. 410-742-8182

Flavors of Italy. 213 E. Main Street. 410-219-9110
Johnny's Sub & Sundae. 1124 E. Main Street. 410-860-5447
Lighthouse II Restaurant. 1502 S. Salisbury Blvd. 410-749-5515
Lombardi's. 315 Civic Center. 410-749-0522
Maynie's Pizzeria. 720 E. College Avenue. 410-749-0744
Mulligan's. 1309 S. Salisbury Blvd. 410-742-6400
Nacho Pete's. 1322 S. Salisbury Blvd. 410-546-0779
Old West Steakhouse. 810 Beaglin Park Drive. 410-548-5775
Phippin's 50 West Restaurant. Rte. 50 West. 410-860-2801
Red Door Sub Shop. 800 S. Salisbury Blvd. 410-742-8294
Round One Bagels. 1147 S. Salisbury Blvd. 410-543-9181
Subrunner's. 901A N. Salisbury Blvd. 410-742-4111
Taylor's Barbecue. 720 E. College Avenue. 410-860-2972
Tia's Tex Mex. 2318 N. Salisbury Blvd. 410-742-9463
Tokyo Steakhouse. 2745 N. Salisbury Blvd.
Tony's Pizza. 917A Snow Hill Road. 410-543-8115
Two Crazy Ladies. 244 Tilghman Road. 410-543-2200
Webster's. 1801 N. Salisbury Blvd. 410-742-8000
Woody's Smokehouse Bar-B-Q. 2625 N. Salisbury Blvd. 410-742-7525

Shopping:

Salisbury Pewter. Rte. 13 North. Tours and pewter for sale
The Country House. 805 East Main Street. "The largest country store in the East".

Fruitland

Fruitland was once part of Lord Baltimore's 6,000 acre estate. When the railroad was established on the Eastern Shore agriculture thrived in the area.

Dining:

Adam's Ribs. 219 N. Fruitland Blvd. 410-749-6961
Angelo's. 411 North Fruitland Blvd. 443-260-0555
Café Portofino. Rte. 13. 410-749-8082
Highway Café. 107 N. Salisbury Blvd. 410-546-9478
Restaurant 213. 213 N. Fruitland Blvd. 410-677-4880
Texas Roadhouse. 107 E. Cedar Lane. 410-677-3660

Pittsville

The town is named for Dr. H.R. Pitts, president of the Wicomico and Pocomoke Railroad that ran between Salisbury and Berlin beginning in 1869.
The restored railroad museum is a museum.

Willards

The town is laid out in a circle with a church, campground and railroad station that once was the post office.

Whaleyville

Whaleyville is believed to be named for Capt. Seth Whaley who came here in the 18th c. Other legends suggest the name came from General Edward Whaley who was a participant in the execution of Charles I and hid out nearby after coming to America. Capt. Peter Whaley (1779-1860) is buried at the Whaley Cemetery off Rte. 346.

Nearby were large cypress swamps. The town was the center of the Pocomoke Swamp shingle industry.

Attractions:

Pullett's Chapel. This 1892 church was built in the Gothic Revival Style and is one of the oldest black churches in Worcester County.

Lewes Corner

Attractions:

Golden Quarter. MD Rte. 376. This private home belonged to the Ayres family and was built before the Revolutionary War.

Fassitt House. MD Rte. 611. This house was built in the 17th c by a follower of Francis Makemie, William Fassitt.

Berlin

Berlin was founded in the 1790's on a 300 acre grant that had become Burley Plantation in 1677, patented by Col. William Stevens. The name is believed to be a contraction of "Burleigh Inn", a tavern at the crossroads of the Philadelphia Post Road and Sinepuxent Road. Commodore Stephen Decatur was born here in 1779. The town was incorporated in 1868. The Reverend Charles Albert Tindley, composer of the song "We Shall Overcome" was born here in 1885.

Main Street has changed little in the last century, although many of the stores are now antique shops rather than other businesses. The movies "Runaway Bride" and "Tuck Everlasting" were filmed here.

Berlin is close to Ocean City and Assateague Island National Seashore. The charm of the town, even though it is away from the beach, should lure the visitor to stay here instead.

Attractions:

Berlin has 47 structures listed in the National Register of Historic Places.

Calvin B. Taylor House Museum. 208 North Main Street. 410-641-1019. Built c1832 this house is now the town museum.

Whaley House (Robin's Nest). 100 West Street. This is the earliest documented dwelling in Berlin, c 1800. Behind the building are a granary, smokehouse and outhouse.

Stevenson-Chandler House. 125 North Main Street. Dates from 1790's.

Kenwood. 101 South Main Street. The house has lovely Federal woodwork.

Telescopic House. 413 South Main Street. Name comes from smaller wing next to larger one.

Waverly. 509 South Main. Federal style house

Pitts-Bounds House. 23 South Main Street. Wrap-around verandah, built 1890's on the site of Burley Inn

Harrison House. Harrison Avenue. Queen Anne style house built in 1890s.

Buckingham Presbyterian Church. Main Street. This is the fourth church to serve the congregation which was organized by Francis Makemie in 1696. This church dates to 1906.

St. Paul's Church. The church was built 1915-16 by African-Americans and is a lovely small brick church.

Calvin B. Taylor Banking Company. Main Street. The bank was established in 1890 and is still located in the same brick building.

Lodging:

Holland House B&B. 5 Bay Street. 410-641-1956. Turn of the century doctor's house.
Atlantic Hotel. 2 North Main Street. 410-641-3589. Charming turn of the century hotel.
Merry Sherwood Plantation. 8909 Worchester Highway. 410-641-2112. The inn is a magnificent 1859 mansion with equally lovely gardens, and is well recommended for a special visit.

Dining:

An Affair to Remember. 104 Pitt Street. 410-629-0707
Drummer's Café. Atlantic Hotel
Assateague Crab House. 7645 Stephen Decatur Highway. 410-641-4330
Rayne's Reef Luncheonette. Main Street.
Goober's Restaurant and Bar. Pitts Street
The King's Pub Restaurant. Commerce Street
Globe Café. Old Globe Theatre. Broad Street. 410-641-9374

Shopping:

Worcester County Arts Council Gallery & Shoppe. Jefferson Street

Assateague Island National Seashore

This island is a 37 mile long barrier reef and was named for the Assateague Indians who inhabited the region. The name means "the marshy or muddy place across". Wild ponies roam the island and a round-up is held annually in July. The ponies were broght by 17th c farmers. The island became a national park in 1965. Over 44 species of mammals and 260 types of birds live on the island.

Attractions:

Barrier Island Visitor Center. Rte 611. 410-641-1441. The center is located south of Ocean City and gives an overview of the area. It is a great attraction for children who can watch a nature film, a hands-on discovery aquarium, a beachcombing exhibit, and gift shop. There are also three nature trails.

Assateague State Park. 7307 Stephen Decatur Highway. 410-641-2120. The park offers special programs, beachcombing, nature walks and canoe trips.

Assateague Island Nature Cruise. 410-289-2700

Ocean City

Ocean City is a favorite resort located on the Atlantic Ocean. The area was first explored by Giovanni de Verrazano who called it "Arcadia". The land was originally deeded to William Wittington in 1771 and was used for livestock grazing.

Ocean City was once a Coast Guard Station. After the Civil War some people patented sand with the name of "The Ladies Resort to the Ocean". The first inn was the Rhode Island Inn built by Isaac Coffin in 1869. In 1875 the Atlantic Hotel was built. The town was incorporated in 1875. Transportation was by stagecoach and ferry. A railroad linked the area to Salisbury beginning in 1876. Most of the hotels were started by women whose husbands were fishermen to earn extra money and provide a place for vacationers. It was known as "The Ladies Resort to the Ocean". The boardwalk was built in the 1880s and became a permanent fixture in 1910. The first automobile bridge was constructed in 1916. The town had been laid out in plats to 32nd Street by 1891 and to 118th Street in 1917. Many of the visitors began coming from Baltimore. In 1925 a fire destroyed much of the boardwalk and many businesses.

The hurricane of August 22, 1933 washed out the railroad and much of the town, including cutting an inlet into Sinepuxent Bay. The first white marlin was caught off Ocean City in 1934 after which it claimed its title as "white Marlin Capital of the World" in 1955. The town was rebuilt and the inlet became a safe harbor. When the Bay Bridge opened in 1952 Ocean City became more easily accessible. Another storm on March 5, 1962 washed away much of the beach and the boardwalk. Today the city remains a resort and deep sea fishing center with 10 miles of beach.

Two of Ocean City's oldest restaurants are the Angler Restaurant founded in 1934 by William Bunting whose father had purchased property to run a fishing business around the turn of the century and Phillips Seafood Restaurants which first began as a seafood shack in 1956 and run by Shirley and Brice Phillips.

Another well known restaurant is the Dough Roller founded in 1980. Dolle's Candyland (1910) and Thrashers French Fries (1922) are also institutions.

Several hotels remain in the same family including the Lankford Hotel built in 1924for the Quillen family, Harrison Hall Hotel built in 1951 for the Harrison family, and the Commander Hotel by the Lynch family. The Beach plaza hotel built in 1954 by Ethel Kelly is now owned by the Phillips family.

Attractions:

Coast Guard Station. Philadelphia Avenue. A Coast Guard station has occupied this site since 1790.

Life-Saving Station Museum

Ocean City Life Saving Station Museum. Boardwalk at Inlet. 410-289-4991. The station was built in 1896. There are exhibits on the history of the U.S. Life-Saving Service, shipwrecks, Ocean City history, bathing suits, the boardwalk, saltwater tanks and a gift shop. From 1875-1915 over 4,500 people were rescued from shipwrecks. . A life saving station was built in 1878 on Caroline Street. he present life saving station was built in 1891 and moved in 1977. in 1915 the life Saving Service became the U.S. Coast Guard. During World War II German U boats were offshore. Several American ships were struck anyway, including the *David Attwater* in 1942.

Model Train Garden. 109 Dorchester Street. Model trains to satisfy every train lover's desires.

Harry W. Kelley Memorial Bridge is named for the eight term mayor in office 1970-85.

Fenwick Island Lighthouse. MD Rte. 528. This was the location of the first Maryland-Delaware boundary marker. A survey was made by John Watson and William Parsons of Pennsylvania. A stone marker dates from 1751.

Frontier Town. Rte. 611. 410-641-0880. The western theme park offers a rodeo, western shops, a steam train, pony rides and other activities.

Herschel-Spelman Carousel. Trimper's Amusement Park. The carousel is one of the oldest operating carousels dating to 1912. Daniel and Margaret Trimper purchased property on the Boardwalk in 1890 and built the park.

The Boardwalk. The boardwalk was built 1900-15. At that time the boards were laid on the sand and stored during the winter. A permanent boardwalk five block was built in 1912 and expanded in the 1920s.

St. Mary's by the Sea Catholic Church. 208 S. Baltimore Avenue. The church was built c1877.

Cloud Dancer Biplane Rides. Rte. 611. 410-641-2484. Ride in an old fashioned biplane.

TheOC Jamboree. Rte. 611. 410-213-7581. Music theater

Ocean City Factory Outlets . Rte. 50

Tea. The Dunes Manor Hotel still serves tea every afternoon in the lobby. 2800 Baltimore Avenue. 410-289-1100

Ice skating. Carousel. 11700 Coastal Highway. 410-524-1000. The Carousel offers ice skating indoors all year round.

Walking maps are available.
Restaurants and lodging are not included in this guide. Please call 1-800-OC-OCEAN for the Ocean City Hotel-Motel-Restaurant Association line.

Bishopville

Just at the Delaware border is Bishopville. Henry Bishop had come to St. Mary's City in 1634. In 1643 he moved to the Eastern Shore. He acquired a patent for 2,300 acres of land in Virginia, but when the Virigina-Maryland border was agreed on his land was found to be in Maryland. A mill operated on the land in the 1700s and was purchased by a Bishop descendant, Littleton Bishop in 1836.

This town was originally known as Milltown. The village was at the damned headwaters of the St. Martin's River. Lumber and farm products were carried from here by boat.

Princess Anne

Princess Anne was created by an Act of the Maryland General Assembly in 1733 and became a port on the Manokin River. Twenty-five acres of "Beckford", a plantation owned by David Brown, were purchased and divided into thirty equal lots with Bridge Street as the main street. The town was named in honor of King George II's daughter. Princess Anne became the Somerset County seat in 1742. After the port silted up the main transportation in was by stagecoach.

Levin Winder served as a major general in the Maryland militia in 1794, speaker of the House of Delegates in 1812 and governor of Maryland 1812-15. When the corner stone of the Washington Monument was laid in 1815 he was grand master of the Masons and presided over the laying of the cornerstone. He died in 1819 and is buried at the family home on Monie Creek.
The first courthouse was built at the corner of Bridge and Broad Streets. This burned in 1832 and the court buildings were moved to Prince William Street.

Attractions:

The town has many lovely buildings and time should be taken for a good walking tour (brochures available). The town owes a great deal to Maude and John Jeffries who restored Tunstall Cottage and then led the effort to preserve the town's architectural history.

Teackle Mansion.11736 Mansion Street. This beautiful neoclassical five-part brick house was built 1802-19 on nine acres for Littleton Dennis Teackle, a merchant, the founder of the Bank of Somerset, railroad investor and statesman, and an associate of Thomas Jefferson's. He is credited with establishing

Maryland's first public school system and the first public commercial bank in the United States. He served in the Maryland House of Delegates from 1824-36.The house was the setting for *The Entailed Hat*, a novel published in 1884 by George Alfred Townsend. The Teackle gatehouse was one of two entrance buildings and housed slave and hired help. The house is undergoing extensive renovations, including returning the rooms to their original colors.

Teackle House

William Geddes House. Broad and Church Streets. The house built c 1755 is the oldest dwelling in Princess Anne.

Charles Jones House. Somerset Avenue. Built 1780 and is located on Lot 3, of the original 30 lots.

Woolford-Elzy House. Somerset Avenue. C 1788

Nutter's Purchase. Flurer's Lane. This small house was built in 1744 as part of a tannery. The land was patented by Christopher Nutter

Linden Hill. Somerset Avenue. C 1835. Lovely Greek Revival home.

John W. Crisfield House. 30556 Somerset Avenue. C 1852 built by US Senator John Crisfield.

Beckford. C 1803 built by John Dennis, former US Senator. The land was originally owned by Judge William Stevens.

Stewart's Neck. Samuel Chase, Signer of the Declaration of Independence, was born here.

St. Andrews Episcopal Church. Church Street. The church was built about 1770 and has been enlarged. This had been the chapel of ease for Almodington. Clayton Torrence wrote *Old Somerset on the Eastern Shore*, while rector here in 1935.

The Somerset County Historical Trust, Inc. Littleton Long House. 11696 Church Street. This Greek Revival 19th c home was moved to its present site in 1996. The house was built c1830 by Littleton Long, a merchant. His son, Charles Chaille-Long became a noted author and African explorer.

University of Maryland Eastern Shore. The university was founded in 1886 by he Delaware conference of the Methodist Church to educate black men and women. It then became the Industrial Branch of Morgan College, and was called Princess Anne Academy. In 1890 it became the Eastern Branch of the Maryland Agricultural College to provide land-grant education to black Maryland citizens. In 1948 the college was renamed Maryland State College, and in 1970 the University of Maryland Eastern Shore.

Boxwood Gardens. Somerset Avenue and Washington Street. The gardens were originally planned by General George Handy (1788-1956) who lived next door. Today the boxwood, crepe myrtle, roses, lilies and other flowers and trees are a treat for the eye and so beautifully maintained.

Somerset Herald. Somerset Avenue. The paper was founded in 1826.

The Mosely Gallery. University of Maryland Eastern Shore.

Manokin Presbyterian Church. The congregation was founded in 1683 by Rev. Francis Makemie. The present structure dates from 1765 and the tower added in 1888.

Manokin Presbyterian Church

Lodging:

The Washington Hotel and Inn. 11784 Somerset Avenue. 410-651-2525. An ordinary (hotel) has operated on this property since 1797.
Hayman House Bed and Breakfast. 30491 Prince William Street. 410-651-1107. This Queen Anne and Colonial Revival home was built in 1898 for Charles H. Hayman who made his fortune from the lumber business.
Waterloo Country Inn. 28822 Mt. Vernon Road. 410-651-0883. This 1750s elegant home was built by Henry Waggaman and restored in 1995. The house is listed in the National Register of Historic Places.
Alexander House Booklovers B&B. 30535 Linden Avenue. 410-651-5195. The house has three literary themed rooms.
Somerset House. 30556 Washington Street. 410-651-4451.
Econo Lodge Motel. Rte. 13. 410-651-9400
Best Value Inn. 30359 Mt. Vernon Road. 410-651-4075
The Richard A. Henson Center. University of Maryland Eastern Shore. 410-651-8100. (Available for groups only)
Traveler's Budget Inn. 30359 Mt. Vernon Road. 410-651-4075

Dining:

Allegro Coffee and Tea Salon. 11775 Somerset Avenue. 410-651-4520
Barbeque Junction. Rte. 13 and Perry Road. 410-651-2776
China Chef. 12087 Somerset Avenue. 410-651-5768
Murphy's Pub. 11782 Somerset Avenue. 410-651-4155
Peaky's Restaurant & Lounge. 30361 Mt. Vernon Road. 410-651-1950
Pizza Plus. 30264 Mt. Vernon Road. 410-651-1200
Sparrow's Pub & Restaurant. 12123 Somerset Avenue. 410-621-0500
Spike's Pub & Subs. 30264 Mt. Vernon Road. 410-651-9124
Snow Biz/Shave Ice. 12100 Carol Lane. 410-651-4548
Mom's Diner. 11724 S. Somerset Avenue. 410-651-0905
Rosa-Nini's Gourmet Ice Cream. 11747 Somerset Avenue. 410-651-3933

Allen

Allen, located on the Wicomico Creek was founded in 1702.

Attractions:

Passerdyke Cottage Museum. The museum has photographs and artifacts from the 19th to 20th c about the area.

Westover

Westover was a shipping point for the Eastern Shore. A number of migrant workers often came here during the summer.

Dining:

Caddy Shack. Great Hope Golf Course. 410-651-5900

Upper Fairmount

Attractions:

Fairmount Academy Historical Association. Academy Grove Historic District. 410-651-0351. By appointment. The academy is comprised of two Italianate two story frame buildings, and was once known as Potato Neck Academy. The school was incorporated by Somerset County in 1867. The school closed in 1969. The association was created to save the school with a 100 year lease. In May of each year the 1800s Festival is held to benefit the Academy.

Kingston

Kingston is named for the King family that amassed a fortune and built a number of large homes in the area. Robert King first settled near King's Creek in 1682. Thomas King Carroll became governor of Maryland in 1830. His daughter, Ella King Carroll, was a member of President Lincoln's cabinet and later became an abolitionist.

Dining:

Joannie's Country Kitchen. 29599 Kingston Lane. 410-623-4111. Breakfast only

Furnace Town

Furnace Town dates from the 1840's. The village is on 22 acres, 16 miles south of Salisbury on Old Furnace Road. John Walter Smith, former governor of Maryland and U.S. Senator, acquired the property in 1912. His family deeded it to the Worcester County Historical Society. This is one of the oldest hot-blast furnaces still intact, and was restored in 1966. The Paul Leifer Nature Trail has paths through the Pocomoke Forest and over the Nassawango Cypress Swamp. For further information contact 410-632-2032.

Nassawango Creek Cypress Swamp

The Nassawango Creek starts near the Delaware line and goes for 18 miles before joining the Pocomoke River. Throughout this region there are bald cypress and black gum swamps. In 1978 E.S. Adkins II gave 157 acres to the

Nature Conservancy to establish the Nassawango Creek Preserve. Today the preserve has over 3,000 acres.

Pocomoke City

Bridge over Pocomoke River

Pocomoke City was settled in the 1600's on the Pocomoke River. The city has had several names, including Stevens Ferry, Warehouse Landing and Newtown. Col. William Stevens served in Cromwell's army in England and came to America only to be shipwrecked at Assateague. He left Virginia in 1660 and came to Maryland. He was the first representative to the General Assembly for Somerset, a deputy governor of Maryland, and a member of Lord Baltimore's council.

The city received its present name in 1878, the year Dr. Isaac Costen was elected the first mayor. The city prospered from shipbuilding. The Tull Shipyards built ocean-going schooners and steamers. Pocomoke City and Snow Hill were the main towns along the Pocomoke River. Other products included shipping of tobacco and lumber; brick manufacturing; and smelting of iron from bog ore found in the swamps during the 1700s and 1800s.

Stephen Handy Long was born in Pocomoke City in 1865, but grew up in Boston. He returned to the Eastern Shore to teach and became the principal of the Pocomoke Grammar School. He became the first African-American school supervisor in Worcester County.

Today sadly, the town has many empty storefronts and vacant homes. Even the boats tied up near the picturesque bridge over the Pocomoke River need some fixing up. The Pocomoke River has been designated a wild and scenic river.

Attractions:

Costen House Museum. Market Street. (410-957-1287). Open Wednesday and Sunday afternoons. The Victorian Italianate building is listed on the National Register of Historic Sites and was the home of Dr. Isaac T. Costen, the first mayor of Pocomoke City. The house and Hall-Walton Memorial Garden are owned and maintained by the Spirit of Newtown Committee.

Beverly of Worcester. MD Rte 371. Donnoch Dennis moved from Virginia in 1669. This private home was constructed in 1774 by his great-grandson Littleton Dennis. The Dennis family was very involved in Maryland and U.S. politics. John Dennis was elected to Congress at the age of 25. He was one of five Federalists who switched their vote to Thomas Jefferson in the presidential election in 1800. John Upshur Dennis exported molasses and cypress and sired 21 children.

Sturgis One-Room School. Front and Willow Streets. 410-947-1913. The only African-American school in Worcester County was built between 1888 and 1900 and operated until 1937. The school was moved to its present site.

Mar-Va Theater. Market Street. (410-957-2423). The theater was built in 1927 and redecorated in 1937. The theater had a separate staircase, ticket booth, bathroom, concession and seating in the balcony for African-Americans.

Pocomoke City Chamber of Commerce. 410-957-1919

Pocomoke City Nature and Exercise Trail. 410-957-1919. The four mile self-guided walk is along the Pcomoke River.

Lodging:

Littleton's B&B. 407 Second Street. 410-957-1645
Puncheon Landing B&B. 33087 Peach Orchard Road. 410-957-4150
Littleton's B&B. Second Street. 410-957-1645
Days Inn. U.S. 13 South. 410-957-3000

Quality Inn. U.S. 13 South. 410-957-1300
Red Carpet Inn. U.S. 13 South. 410-957-1029
Holiday Inn Express. Rte. 13 at MD Rte. 756. 410-957-6444

Dining:

Upper Deck Restaurant & Lounge. U.S. 13 South. 410-957-3166
Traders Fried Chicken, Ribs & BBQ. Ames Plaza. 410-957-1682

Uniontown

Uniontown was founded as an African-American community. Lt. Col. Edward P. Drummond entered the last class of pilots to train at the Tuskegee Army Air Field in Alabama. He spent over 25 years in the U.S. Air Force flying in Korea and Vietnam.

Newark

Attractions:

Queponco Railroad Station. 410-641-0067. The station was erected in 1910 on the rail line between Berlin and Snow Hill. The building was sold in the 1960s and became a museum in 1999.

Snow Hill

Snow Hill was settled in 1642 by colonists from the "Snow Hill" section of London on the banks of the Pocomoke River. Col. William Stevens of Rehoboth had patented a tract here in 1676. Col. Stevens sold the lad to Henry Bishop in 1685. The town received its charter in 1686 and was made a Royal Port in 1694 by King William and Queen Mary of England. The town exported cypress lumber and tobacco, and was known for its shipbuilding. It sits on the highest navigable point of the Pocomoke River.

The first Presbyterian Church in America was founded in Snow Hill in 1684 by Francis Makemie. In 1742 Snow Hill became the county seat of Worcester County. In 1793 the town was platted into 100 lots by Joshua Mitchell. As a port it served the western shore and was on the route to the Nassawango Iron Furnace that produced bog iron. Ships traveling between Norfolk and Baltimore use the Pocomoke River and Snow Hill as a port. The Richardson, Smith and Moore Lumber Company became the largest employer.

Following the Civil War railroads were built along the Eastern Shore and the river lost its prominence for transportation. The shipyards and boarding homes closed up. However the population turned to agriculture growing corn, soybeans and livestock. The timber business is still important and Paul M. Jones Co. still operates in the town.

A few years ago when many of the shops closed, local merchants rallied to find alternative uses for them. Snow Hill is now billed as "The Antiques Capital of the Eastern Shore".

William Julius "Judy" Johnson was born in Snow Hill in 1899 and went on to play baseball in the Negro League. He was inducted into the National Baseball Hall of Fame in 1975. The Legionnaire Stars baseball team was formed in 1945 as a segregated team.

Attractions:

The town has many lovely homes including a number of Federal style houses. In 1893 a fire destroyed much of the downtown area, including records in the Courthouse. A walking tour is recommended (Maps available). The annual house tour is in September.

Worcester County Courthouse. Market Street. The first was built 1742 and burned 1834. The present courthouse was built in 1894.

The Julia A. Purnell Museum. 208 W. Market Street. 410-632-0515. Open April to October and by appointment. Julia Purnell made over 1000 needlepoint pictures. With the help of her son this museum was founded in 1942 to preserve many of these masterpieces. The museum also traces the history of Snow Hill. The building was originally a Catholic Church, built as part of the Wilmington Archdiocese in 1892.

Mount Zion One-Room Schoolhouse Museum. Ironshire Street. 410-632-1265. This building is maintained by the Worcester County Teachers Association.

Makemie United Presbyterian Church. American Presbyterianism was established in 1683 by Francis Makemie. The present church was built in 1889.

Johnson House. 106 E. Market Street. This house once known as King's Necessity, dates to 1784 with later additions added.

Thebaud Cottage. 201A E. Market Street. This cottage is also known as "The Little House" and dates c 1800.

211 E. Market. This building dates to 1793 and housed the first telephone office in Snow Hill.

Chanceford. 209 W. Federal. This Greek revival building was built between 1759 and 1795.

King's Necessity. 106 E. Market Street. This house dates to 1784 with later additions added.

Corddry Company Crossing. Washington and River Streets. 410-632-3971. The building houses a model train exhibit.

All Hallows Episcopal Church. Market Street. The church was established in 1692. The present structure dates from 1756. The bible was a gift from Queen Anne in 1701. Many old families are buried here including Upshurs and Wilmers.

All Hallow's Episcopal Church

Cellar House. On Pocomoke River. This plantation house dates back to the 1730s. However the land grant dates from 1661 given by Lord Baltimore.

The Phillips House. 300 W. Market Street. The house between 1740-50.

Mumford House. 207 W. Ironshire. Mumford House was built in 1790. It has a gambrel roof, cypress board exterior and a summer kitchen.

Salem. 310 Park Row. Salem was erected c 1764. In the front yard is a Bicentennial Tree.

MacPherson House. 100 N. Washington. This Federal style house dates to c 1800.

The Phillips House. This Georgian house was built c 1740-50.

Gov. John Walter Smith House. 104 S. Church Street. The Queen anne Victorian is a gracious large house.

Ebenezer United Methodist Church. The church was built in 1899.

Lodging:

Chanceford Hall Inn. 209 W. Federal Street. 410-632-2231. 18th century Greek revival home.
Snow Hill Inn B&B. 104 E. Market Street. 410-632-2102. This is both an inn and restaurant.
River House Inn. 201 E. Market Street. 410-632-2722. The lovely 1860s Victorian house sits on two acres overlooking the Pocomoke River.

Dining:

Bailey's Café. 104 Green Street. 410-632-3704
Snow Hill Inn & Restaurant. 104 E. Market Street. 410-632-2101

Girdletree

Attractions:

Girdletree Barnes Bank Museum. 410-632-1641. The bank was built by George Barnes in 1902. The bank closed in the 1930s and was restored in 1999.

Public Landing

Public Landing, located on the Chincoteague Bay, was once a summer resort. Mansion House was for many years a hotel.

Attractions:

Mansion House. MD Rte. 365. This private home was built by the Spence family.

Showell

Samuel Showell was known to have been here in 1689. In the 1800s Lemuel Showell brought the railroad here and built a resort. He was president of the Wicomico and Pocomoke Railroad. The town had been called St. Martin's. The Showell family supposedly had a large number of slaves. However no record of slaves held by the family has ever been found.

Attractions:

St. Martin's Episcopal Church. This 44 by 54 foot structure was built in 1756 by James Johnson.

Rehobeth

Rehobeth was named for the plantation owned by Colonel William Stevens on a tract he patented in 1665 near the Pocomoke River. He may once have owned as many as 20,000 acres. Col. Stevens established the first ferry on the Pocomoke River. Even though he was a member of the Church of England he applied to the Presbytery of Laggan for a minister. Francis Makemie became the pastor. Rev. Makemie also went on to organize the Presbytery of Philadelphia. Rehobeth is a Biblical name meaning "There is Room".

Attractions:

Rhehobeth Presbyterian Church. Rte. 406 outside Crisfield. The church is the oldest Presbyterian Church in the United States, built in 1706 by Reverend Francis Makemie, "Father of the American Presbyterian Church.

Old Coventry Church. This Episcopal Church is now in ruins. The first church was built here about 1697.

Marion

Land for a town was donated by John Horsey with the arrival of the railroad. The town is named for his daughter. In the early 1900s Marion, Maryland was the largest shipper of strawberries in the world! Hundreds of refrigerated railroad cars left the Marion Train Station each day. Sadly by the 1950s the industry died out. Corn and soy beans took over as dominant crops in this lower part of the Eastern Shore of Maryland.

Attractions:

Accohannock Indian Tribal Museum. 28380 Crisfield-Marion Road. 410-623-2973

Eastern Shore Early Americana Museum. 30195 Rehobeth Road. 410-623-8324

Marion Station Railroad Museum & Gift Shoppe. 28380 Crisfield-Marion Road. 410-623-2420

Colbourne Creek. MD Rte.357. Stephen Horsey was the first known settler in Maryland below the Choptank River. He patented the Colbourne tract in 1663. He had first come to Virginia in 1643 and in 1652 became a member of the Committee of Six that drafted the *Northampton Protest*. This document opposed taxation of the Eastern Shore settlers without representation in the Virginia Assembly. He was arrested several times for refusing to pay taxes to support the Church of England. In about 1661 he moved to Maryland.

Crisfield

Far down the Eastern Shore is Crisfield, still home to many watermen. The town was originally named Annemessex, the Algonquin name meaning "Bountiful Waters". South of here lies Cedar Island Wildlife Management Area that Capt. John Smith named Watkins' Point in 1612. Maryland and Virginia have often argued over this point as the Maryland Charter established this point in the Chesapeake Bay as the dividing line between the two provinces.

In 1666 Benjamin Summers was given a land grant by Lord Baltimore. Three hundred acres were surveyed and it was given the name Annemesex, an area that now borders the present site of Somers Cove.

This was an agricultural area and then fishing became important. The town was renamed Somers Cove, and later named for John Woodland Crisfield (1808-97), a lawyer and former congressman, who financed the Eastern Shore Railroad. In 1854 when a Coast and Geodetic survey of the Chesapeake Bay found large number of oyster beds in Tangier Sound, Crisfield found itself on the map. In 1868 the Eastern Shore Railway built a terminal in Crisfield. Seafood could now be transported more quickly and refrigerated. Crisfield was then called the "Seafood Capital of the World".

Albert LaVallette settled on Hammock Point and cultivated terrapin by using waste from crab pickings. He eventually went to Philadelphia and other cities touting his "LaVallette Diamondback Terrapin", his own recipe for terrapin stew. By signing contracts with only the most exclusive restaurants, he made a killing on selling terrapin. Soon the Bay was depleted of almost all terrapin and the Maryland legislature passed laws to protect them. In the meantime Mr. LaVallette had made his fortune and built a large home in Crisfield. Isaac Solomon who had patented a pasteurizing canning process, brought his ideas to Crisfield and set up a processing plant here. By 1910 the Crisfield Customs House had the largest registry of sailing vessels in the U.S.

Harbor at Crisfield

Harry Clifton Byrd was born near Crisfield. He developed the University of Maryland into a well-known institution.

Charles D. Briddell, a blacksmith from Shelltown, moved to Crisfield and began producing shucking knives, oyster tongs, mallets and products for the seafood industry. His company Carvel Hall survived until just recently.

The Tawes' family was in the seafood, ice-packing and banking business. Governor J. Millard Tawes served as the 54th governor of the State of Maryland. He created the Center for Public Broadcasting and was the first Southern governor to ban discrimination in public accommodations and state employment. He started the University of Maryland Baltimore campus, authorized the second span of the Bay Bridge, and served as the first secretary of the Department of Natural Resources. After serving as governor he returned to Crisfield.

Lem and Steve Ward were the premiere decoy carvers in the United States. Raised in Crisfield they were asked to enter the New York Decoy Show in 1948. The brothers won "Best in Show" and in other categories. Their workshop has been preserved, along with the barbershop they operated on Sackertown Road. After their deaths the buildings deteriorated until 1993 when wildlife artist Jack Schroeder formed Homeplace, Inc. to restore them. The Crisfield Heritage Foundation now maintains the buildings.

On March 29, 1928 a fire broke out at the Odd Fellows Hall on Main Street. Over 90 buildings were burned. Today most of the canning and processing facilities are closed down. The town has experienced some lean times, and now depends on seafood festivals and other promotions, plus the building of expensive condominiums and revitalization of downtown.

Attractions:

Makepeace. Built in 1663, this old home overlooks Johnson's Creek. John Roach received a patent for this tract in 1663.

Ward Brothers' Workshop. 3195 Sackertown Road. Open by appointment. 410-968-2501. The workshop of Lem and Steve Ward, famous decoy carvers, has been restored by Homeplace and has been given to the Crisfield Heritage Foundation.

J. Millard Tawes Historical Museum, Visitors' Center & Gift Shop. Somers Cove Marina. 3 Ninth Street. 410-968-2501. Honors Gov. J. Millard Tawes (1894-1979) who was a native of Crisfield. Somers Cove Marina is a $30 million development on a farm founded in 1663 by Benjamin Somers. Recently the museum has offered ElderHostel stays to encourage tourism in Crisfield.

The Gov. Tawes Library. 410-968-2501. Open by appointment. The 1887 Victorian house was the childhood home of Gov. Tawes and is listed on the National Register of Historic Places. Gov. Tawes created the Center for Public Broadcasting, was the first southern governor to ban discrimination in public facilities, and started the University of Maryland Baltimore campus. He authorized the second span of the Chesapeake Bay Bridge and served as the first secretary of the Department of Natural Resources.

Crockett House. Main Street. 1888. Historic Victorian home

Eco-Tours. W. Main Street and Crisfield City Dock. 410-968-9870

Smith Island Cruises. City Dock. 410-425-2771.

Tangier Island/Chesapeake Bay Cruises. City Dock. 410-968-2338

Cedar Island Marsh Sanctuary. 3 Ninth Street. 410-968-2501

Somerset County Arts Council. 26430 Burton Avenue. 410-968-2787. Art and jewelry are sold here, in addition to classes.

Janes Island State Park. 26280 Alfred Lawson Drive. 410-968-1565. Fishing, birdwatching, trails, campsites, launch ramps

Lodging:

The Cove. 218 Broadway. 410-425-2771
Bea's B&B. 10 S. Somerset Avenue. 410-968-0423. The house was built in 1909 by John Handy, founder of the Handy Soft Shell Crab Company.
Paddlewheel Motel. 701 West Main Street. 410-968-2220
The Pines Motel. 127 N. Somerset Avenue. 410-968-0900
My Fair Lady B&B. 38 West Main Street. 410-968-0532
Best Value Inn. 700 Robert Norris Drive. 410-968-1900
Nan N Pop's Bed, Breakfast & More. 315 W. Main Street. 410-968-3535

Restaurants:

Original Captain's Galley. Main Street and City Dock. 410-968-3313
Café at the Pottery. 952 West Main Street. 410-968-9040
Dockside 2 Restaurant. 1003 W. Main Street. 410-968-2800
Waterman's Inn. 901 W. Main Street. 410-968-2119
Circle Inn Restaurant. 4012 Crisfield Highway. 410-968-1969
Captain's Carry-out. 945 Main Streets. 410-968-1305
Side Street Seafood Market & Restaurant. 204 S. Tenth Street. 410-968-2442
Gordon's Confectionery. 831 W. Main Street. 410-968-0566

Ice Cream Gallery. 5 Goodsell Alley. 410-968-0809
Oriental Jade. 103 N. 4th Street. 410-968-3888
Peppy's Italian and Seafood Restaurant. 821 W. Main Street. 410-968-2727
Pizza Shoppe. 57 Richardson Avenue. 410-968-0333
Puff's Place. 4459 Crisfield Highway. 410-968-3218
Cove Restaurant. 718 Broadway. 410-968-9532
Tropical Chesapeake. 712 Broadway. 410-968-3622

Holland Island

About ten miles north of Smith Island is a 75 acre marshy island called Holland Island. The island once had a population of 350 people, but has now eroded to these few acres. Stephen White, a developer and former Methodist minister, is attempting to stop this erosion at his own expense and with his own equipment.

Smith Island

Smith Island was visited by Capt. John Smith who explored the Chesapeake in 1608. The island was settled in 1657. In 1679 Henry Smith purchased 1,000 acres on the island and it is named for him.

Farmers settled the island in the 17th c. Over 50 skipjacks once operated from here. Watermen still provide the bounty of the Chesapeake to a co-op for crab that runs May to October. After picking these crabs they are sent to Crisfield by boat.

Smith Island is about 12 miles west of Crisfield and can be reached by ferry leaving Crisfield at 12:30. The island has lost over 1200 acres to the Bay, but three main communities are located here – Ewell, Tylerton, and Rhodes Point. The land was used mainly for raising sheep and cattle. Later the island became known for its seafood. Many of the same families are still here, often speaking a dialect that even "mainlanders' have trouble understanding. The island's religious roots revolve around the Methodist faith, and "camp meetings" are a yearly event. No liquor is allowed to be sold on the island, even though the Driftwood General Store has been trying for many years to get a license. Religion still prevails. The population of the island is about 350.

Attractions:

Smith Island Center. 20846 Caleb Jones Road. Ewell. 410-425-3351. The visitor center and museum trace the history of Smith Island.

Martin's National Wildlife Refuge. Caleb Jones Road. Ewell. 410-425-4971

Smith Island Crabmeat Co-op, Inc. 21128 Wharf Street. Tylerton. 410-425-2035

William B. Mullins Education Center. Chesapeake Bay Foundation. 21151 Marshall Street. Ewell. 410-968-1902

Lodging:

Inn of Silent Music.2955 Tyler Road. Tylertown. 410-425-3541
Ewell Tide Inn. 4063 Tyler Road. Ewell. 410-425-2141
Smith Island Motel. 4025 Smith Island Road. Ewell. 410-425-3321
Chesapeake Fishing Adventures. Tylerton. 410-968-0175
Whisper Island Retreat. 4026 Tyler Road. 410-968-3456

Dining:

Rukes. 20840 Caleb Jones Road. Ewell. 410-425-2311
Bayside Inn. 4065 Smith Island Road. Ewell. 410-425-2771
Drum Point Market. 21162 Center Street. Tylerton. 410-425-2108
Nan-N-Pop's Place. 21148 Tuff Street. Ewell. 410-968-0840

Parson Island

Parson Island was named for Joshua Thomas "Parson of the Islands". The island was bought by McCormick and Co. in 1944 for a spice experimentation and conference center.

Camping

Martinak State Park. 137 Deep Shore Road. Denton. 410-820-1668
Tuckahoe State Park. 13070 Crouse Hill Road. Queen Anne. 410-820-1668
Duck Neck Campground. Chestertown. 410-778-3070
Lake Bonnie Campsites, Inc. Rte. 313. Goldsboro. 410-482-8479
Holiday Park. 14620 Drapers Mill Road. Greensboro. 410-482-6797

Sandy Hill Family Camp. Quantico. 410-873-2471
Princess Anne Campground. U.S. Rte. 13. Princess Anne. 410-651-1520
Eagle's Nest. 12612 Eagle's Nest Road. Berlin. 410-213-0097
Roaring Point Waterfront Campground. Nanticoke. 410-873-2553
Taylor's Island Family Campground. Bayshore Road. Taylor's Island. 410-397-3275
Tideland Park Campground. Taylor's Island. 410-397-3473
Janes Island State Park. Crisfield. 410-968-1565
Lake Somerset Campground. Westover. 410-957-1866
Somers Cove Marina. 715 Broadway. Crisfield. 410-968-0925
Goose Creek Marina. Upper Fairmount. 410-651-1193
Woodlawn Campground. Delmar
Madison Bay Marina & Campground. Rte. 16, Madison. 410-228-4111
Smith Island Marina. Ewell. 410-968-3309
Bay Country Campground. Rte. 445. Rock Hall. 410-639-7485
Duck Neck Campground. Chestertown. 410-778-3070
Holiday Park Campground. Greensboro. 410-482-6797
Assateague Island National Seashore. Berlin. 410-641-3030
Assateague State Park. Berlin. 410-641-2120
Bali-Hi RV Park. Bishopville. 410-352-5477
Ft. Whaley Campground. Whaleyville. 410-641-9785
Frontier Town Campground. Berlin. 410-641-0880
Ocean City Campground. 105 70th Street. Ocean City. 410-525-7601
Pocomoke River State Park. Snow Hill. 410-632-2566

Bed and Breakfast Associations

Bed & Breakfast of Maryland. 410-269-6232
Dorchester County Bed & Breakfast Consortium. Listed by individual B&Bs
Gracious Inns of the Chesapeake. 410-778-3970. For Chestertown area

Chapter Four

Eastern Shore Boats

Yachts, Workboats and other Sailing Vessels

The Chesapeake Bay and its many creeks and rivers make this a perfect location to start a journey to, keep your boat here or just enjoy the thrill of taking a ride on someone else's. Almost everyone owns a boat, whether it is a sailboat, workboat, or some other means of transportation.

Log Canoe *Island Bird*

The Indian dugout log canoe with a sail was the earliest boat. Later, the settlers used this same style boat. The racing canoe is thought to have been introduced by Robert D. Lambdin of St. Michael's in the mid 1800s. The log canoes are often referred as "butterflies of the sea". On summer week-ends one can watch these race against each other on the various Eastern Shore rivers. They are an incredible sight with a mass of sail. Three famous trophies are now vied for each year: The Governor's Cup, the John B. Harrison trophy, and the William Sidney Covington Memorial Trophy. The William A. Baker Award was presented by the Mystic Seaport Museum to the log canoe owners of the Chesapeake Bay in

1992. This hangs at the Chesapeake Bay Maritime Museum in St. Michael's. Twenty-one log canoes survive, but only about 10 actively race.

In the late 1800s another type of canoe, the brogan, was carved from 5 logs, pointed at each end, and larger than the log canoe. These were about 40 feet long and had two masts raked back, each with a triangular sail. It also carried a jib and a cabin.

The bugeye is a two-master schooner descended from the canoe, and was used for oystering in shallow waters, beginning the 1860s. These were made from 7 logs. Almost 600 bugeyes were produced, about half built near Crisfield.

The pungy (pongee or oyster boat) was a bit larger and carried topmasts. The schooner rigs were descended from the Baltimore clippers and were used for dredging oysters.

The scow is a flat-bottomed sailing craft with a square bow and stern. The boats were later rigged as schooners and sloops. They hauled grain, fish and salt. Gunners used them as houseboats.

Skipjack

Sloops in the U.S. date back to when Captain John Smith first explored the Chesapeake Bay in this type of vessel. During the Revolution and War of 1812 sloops plied the waters of the Chesapeake and were noted for their speed against the larger British ships. The ships were also used for trading and in the mid

1800s to transport oysters. Some were used as dredgers for oystering and others as "buy boats". These were later to be replaced by the skipjack.

The skipjack has a single raked mast and centerboard. Over 2,000 skipjacks worked the Bay waters with the oyster catch peaking at 15 million bushels in 1884. Skipjacks dredge by law for oysters under sail Wednesday through Friday and use of a push boat on Mondays and Tuesdays. Only a few skipjacks dredge now due to the depleted oyster beds. The others lay rotting or destroyed.

A patent tonger is a vessel that uses hydraulically powered oyster tongs to retrieve the oysters. Hand tongers do the same thing with muscle powered rake shafts. The season is September 15-March 31.

Workboats have been built on the Eastern Shore for crabbers, oystermen and fishermen. These hearty wooden boats are simple in design and may range from sixteen feet to more than 30 feet.

Workboat *Elsie B* of Tilghman Island

The catboat is native to New England, but a number have been built on the Eastern Shore. These boats range from 12 feet to more than 25 feet. These gaft-rigged boats can often be spotted around Tilghman Island where Maynard Lowery has built quite a number.

Sadly, gone are the Chesapeake Appreciation Days and other events that hosted many of these traditional boats. However, skipjack and log canoe races still thrill any beholder, and are held at various times during the summer in different towns.

Ferries and Steamboats

Whitehaven Ferry

Travel to the other side of the Chesapeake was limited to ferries, steamships or other types of vessels until 1952 with the opening of the Bay Bridge. In the 1760's innkeeper Samuel Middleton operated a ferry from Annapolis across the bay carrying people and horses. Packet sloops were used to cross the Chesapeake, the main one running between Annapolis and Rock Hall. These sloops carried passengers and freight. Other ferries ran between Oxford and Annapolis, St. Michael's and Wye Landing.

The first steamboats were put into operation in 1813. The *Chesapeake's* captain was Edward Trippe of Dorchester County. The *Emma Giles* carried passengers to resorts such as Tolchester Beach and Betterton. In 1919 the 201 foot side-wheeler *Governor Emerson C. Harrington* made the Annapolis-Claiborne run with cars and passengers in just a little over an hour.

An even larger vessel, the double-ended *Governor Albert C. Ritchie,* was launched in 1926. The *John M. Dennis* was put into service in 1929 and the terminus was moved from Claiborne to Matapeake, making the crossing in about 45 minutes, and costing 50 cents round trip! The trip from Annapolis was from the King George Street dock. In 1943 this was moved to Sandy Point now taking only 25 minutes. The *Dennis* made its last crossing in 1952 when the Bay Bridge opened. In June 1973 the second Chesapeake Bay Bridge span opened, one year late and cost $60 million more than the $65 million estimate!

Ferry boats are unique to the rivers of the Eastern Shore. A rope crosses the river pulling the flat-bottomed scow. The course of the ferry is guided by a steel cable attached to the port side of the boat. These boats usually carry three cars. The Whitehaven Ferry and Upper Ferry on the Wicomico River still use this method. A larger ferry crosses from Oxford to Bellevue. This ferry has been in use since 1683, although the new ferry uses power, not a cable.

Lighthouses/Lightships

Along the Eastern Shore are quite a few of lighthouses. By 1850 there were 21 lighthouses in the Chesapeake Bay and 9 lightships. Among the most unique of the lighthouses built were the screwpile type.

Lighthouses on the Eastern Shore include:

- Bloody Point Bar is located near the southern tip of Kent Island. This was constructed in 1882 at a cost of $25,000. The tower stood 56 feet. In 1960 a fire destroyed the lighthouse. A lighthouse still stands here.

- Hooper Strait Lighthouse was located on Hooper Strait between Bloodsworth Island and Hooper Island and Bishops Head. The Hooper Strait Lightship was built in 1827 at a cost of $8,500 by William Price of Baltimore and put in service in 1828 with Richard F. Fox as the first keeper. He was replaced in 1829 by John Hooper who was keeper until 1839, when he was replaced by Robert Griffith, the last keeper. William Easby of Alexandria, Virginia constructed a second lightship in 1845. A screwpile lighthouse was built here in 1867, but was carried away by an ice mass in 1877. A new lighthouse was built in 1879 and the light automated in 1954. Today the lighthouse has been moved to the Chesapeake Bay Maritime Museum in St. Michael's.

- Sharps Island light is near the southern tip of Tilghman Island. It was named after Peter Sharpe, a Quaker who owned it before 1675. The first lighthouse was built in 1838. In 1866 a screwpile lighthouse was built, but destroyed by ice floes in 1881. The present lighthouse dates from 1882.

- Hooper Island light was built near Hooper Island in 1901.

- Solomons Lump is in Kedge Strait north of Smith Island. The first light was built in 1875 and crushed by ice in 1893. The lighthouse was replaced in 1895 and automated in 1950.

- Cape Charles Lighthouse on Smith Island was built in 1828. In 1856 Congress appropriated money to build a new tower, but construction was later halted during the Civil War. This was completed in 1864. A third lighthouse was built in 1894.

- Turkey Point Lighthouse. North East.

Marine Information

Harbor Master, Cambridge. 410-228-4031
Maryland Marine Police. 911
United States Coast Guard. 410-267-8107
Weather Service. 301-936-1212
Department of Natural Resources. 410-260-8200

Bridge Opening Schedules

Knapps Narrows. Tilghman Island. On demand
Kent Narrows. Kent Island. May 1-October 31. Open on hour and half-hour
Cambridge. On demand

Special Yachting Events

Log canoe races take place on the Eastern Shore June to September.
Skipjack races are held on Deal Island in September.
The Volvo Around the World Race

Yacht Clubs

Cambridge Yacht Club. Mill Street, Cambridge. 410-228-2141
Miles River Yacht Club. Long Haul Creek, St. Michael's. 410-745-8589
The Oxford Yacht Club. 502 E. Strand, Oxford. 410-226-5450
Tred Avon Yacht Club. Oxford. 410-226-5269
Tilghman-on-Chesapeake. Tilghman Island. 410-886-2300
Sassafras River Yacht Club. Georgetown
Kent Island Yacht Club. Chester. 410-643-4101
Wicomico Yacht Club. Allen. 410-219-5248
Green Hill Yacht and Country Club. On Wicomico River. 410-749-5119

Towing/Recovery

Generation III Marina. Cambridge. 410-228-2520
Tow Jamm Marine, Inc. Neavitt. 410-745-3000
SeaTow. Kent Narrows. 410-267-7650

Marinas/Docks

Accredited Yacht Services. 442 Kent Narrows Way North. Grasonville. 410-827-8838
Angler's Restaurant & Marina. 3015 Kent Narrows S. Grasonville. 410-827-6717
Bahia Marina, 22nd Street, Ocean City. 410-289-7438
Bates Marina.106 Richardson Street. Oxford. 410-226-5105
Bay Bridge Marina. 357 Pier One Road. Stevensville. 410-643-3162
Bob Dolbey. Whitehaven. 410-543-2626
Bohemia Anchorage. Glebe Road. Earleville. 410-275-8148
Bohemia Bay Yacht Harbour. 1026 Town Point Road. Chesapeake City. 410-885-2601
Bohemia Vista Yacht Basin. 140 Vista Marina Road. Chesapeake City. 410-885-5402
Cambridge Marine. 301 Muir Street. Cambridge. 410-228-4820
Cambridge Municipal Yacht Basin. Warer Street. Cambridge. 410-228-4031
Cambridge Yacht Club. Water Street. Cambridge. 410-228-2141
Campbell's Bachelor Point Yacht Co. 26106A Bachelors Harbor. Oxford. 410-226-5592
Campbell's Town Creek Boatyard. 109 Myrtel Avenue. Oxford. 410-226-0213
Castle Harbor Marina. 301 tackle Circle. Chester. 410-643-5599

Cedar Hill Marina. Bivalve
Chester River Marine Services. 7501 Church Hill Road. Chestertown. 410-778-2240
Chestertown Marina. 410-778-3616
Crockett Brothers Boatyard. 202 Banks Street. Oxford. 410-226-5113
Deckelman's Long Cove Marina. Rte. 288. Rock Hall. 410-778-6777
Droter's Angler's Marina. 3015 Kent Narrows Way. Grasonville. 410-827-6717
Duffy Creek Marina. 20 Duffy Creek Road. Georgetown. 410-275-2141
East Side Seafood Company. 201 Trenton Street. Cambridge. 410-228-9007
Gateway Marina and Ship's Store. 1606 Marina Drive. Trappe. 410-476-3304
Generation III Marina. 205 Cedar Street, Cambridge. 410-228-2520
Georgetown Yacht Basin. Georgetown. 410-648-5112
Gootee's Marine. 1439 Hoopers Island Road. Church Creek. 410-397-3122
Granary Marina. George Street. Fredericktown. 410-648-5112
Gratitude Marina. Rock Hall. 410-639-7011
Great Oak Marina. Great Oak. 410-778-5007
Green Point Marina. Worton. 410-778-1615
Gregg Neck Boat Yard. Georgetown. 410-648-5360
Hacks Point Marina. 1645 Glebe Road. Hacks Point. 410-275-8995
Harbour North Marina. 111 River Road. Chesapeake City. 410-885-5656
Harrison's. 21551 Chesapeake House Drive. Tilghman. 410-886-2121
Haven Harbour Marina. MD Rte. 20 and Swan Creek, Rock Hall. 410-778-6697
Hill's Marina. Rock Hall. 410-639-7267
Hyatt Regency. 100 Heron Blvd. Cambridge. 410-233-1234
Island View Marina. 1814 Crab Alley Drive, Chester. 410-643-2842
Kennersley Point Marina. 223 Marina Lane. Church Hill. 410-758-2394
Kentmorr Harbour Marina. 910 Kentmorr Road, Stevensville. 410-643-0029
Knapp's Narrows Marina & Yacht Center. Tilghman. 410-886-2720
Lankford Bay Marina. 23002 McKinleyville Road. Rock Hall. 410-778-1414
Lippincott Marine. 3420 Main Street, Grasonville. 410-827-9300
Long Cove Marina. Route 288. Rock Hall. 410-778-6777
Long Point Marina. 125 Kitty Knight Blvd. Earleville. 410-275-8181
Losten Marina. 1645 Glebe Road. Earleville. 410-275-8186
Marina Bay Sea & Sea. Madison Canning Road. Madison. 410-228-4111
Mears Point Marina. 428 Kent Narrows Way N. Grasonville. 410-827-8888
Mears Yacht Haven. 502 E. Strand, Oxford. 410-226-5450
North Point Marina. 5639 Walnut Street. Rock Hall. 410-639-2907
Ocean City Fishing Center. 1-800-322-3065
Ocean Pines Swim and Racquet Club. Seabreeze Road. 410-641-7447
Ocean Pines Yacht Club Marina. Mumford's Landing. Ocean Pines. 410-641-7447
Oxford Boatyard. 402 E. The Strand, Oxford. 410-226-5101
Osprey Point Yacht Club & Marina. 20786 Rock Hall Avenue. Rock Hall. 410-639-2663

Pelorus Marina, Inc. Rock Hall. 410-639-2663
Piney Narrows Yacht Haven. 500 Piney Narrows Road. Chester. 410-643-6600
Port of Salisbury. 506 West Main Street. Salisbury. 410-548-3176
Queen Anne Marina. 412 Congressional Drive. Grasonville. 410-643-2021
Richmond's Marina. 14 Greenspring Road. 410-275-2061
Rippons Harbor. 1814 Hoopersville Road. Hoopersville. 410-397-3200
Rock Hall Landing Marina. Sharp Street. Rock Hall. 410-639-2224
Rock Hall Marina Railway. Rock Hall. 410-639-2263
Rolph's Wharf Marina. 1008 Rolph's Wharf Road. Chestertown. 410-778-6389
Sailing Associates. 78 George Street. Fredericktown. 410-275-8171
Sailing Emporium, Inc. 21144 Green Lane, Rock Hall. 410-778-1342
St. Michael's Harbour Inn & Marina. 101 N. Harbor Road, St. Michael's. 410-745-9001
St. Michael's Town Dock Marina, Inc. 305 Mulberry Street, St. Michael's. 410-745-2400
Sassafras Harbor Marina. 2 George Street. Georgetown. 410-275-1144
Schaefer's Canal House. 208 Bank Street. Chesapeake City. 410-885-2204
Schooners Llanding. Oxford. 410-226-0160
Scotchman's Creek Marina. 34 Greenspring Road. Earleville. 410-275-2631
Scott Marine Service. 3212 Main Street. Grasonville. 410-827-8150
Scott's Cove Marina. Chance. 410-784-2428
Scott's Point Marina. 215 Front Street. Chestertown. 410-778-2959
Sea & Sea Marina. Madison. 410-228-4111
Severn Marine Services. Tilghman Island. 410-886-2159
Skipjack Cove. 150 Skipjack Cove Road. Fredericktown. 410-275-2122
Skipjack Landing Marina. 1804 Crab Alley Road. Chester. 410-643-2694
Somers Cove Marina. Crisfield. 410-968-0925
Spring Cove Marina. Rock Hall. 410-639-2110
Steamboat Landing Marina. Rock Hall. 410-639-7212
Sunset Marina. Ocean City. 410-213-9600
Swan Creek Marina, Inc. 6043 Lawton Avenue, Rock Hall. 410-639-7813
Talbot Street Pier. 311 Talbot Street. Ocean City. 410-289-9125
Taylor's Island Marina. Rte. 16. Taylor's Island. 410-221-2911
Tilghman Island Marina. 410-886-2979
Tolchester Marina. 410-778-1400
Two Rivers Yacht Basin. 64 Two Rivers Lane. Chesapeake City. 410-885-2257
Wharf at Handy's Landing. Worton. 410-778-4363
Whitehaven Marina. 410-873-2626
Worton Creek Marina. 23145 Buck Neck Road. Worton. 410-778-3282
Yacht Maintenance. 101 Hayward Street. Cambridge. 410-228-8878
Somers Cove Marina. Crisfield. 410-968-0925
Goose Creek Marina. Upper Fairmount. 410-651-1193
Smith Island Marina. Ewell. 410-968-3309

Boatyards/Repairs

Crockett Brothers Boatyard, Inc. 202 Bank Street, Oxford. 410-226-5113
Oxford Boatyard. 402 E. The Strand, Oxford. 410-226-5101
Dockside Boat Works. 11791 Cordova Road. Cordova. 410-820-1612
Campbell's Bachelor Point Yacht Co. 26106A Bachelors Harbor. Oxford. 410-226-5592
Higgins Yacht Yard. St. Michael's. 410-745-9303
Campbell's Town Creek Boatyard. 109 Myrtel Avenue. Oxford. 410-226-0213
Generation III Marina. 205 Cedar Street, Cambridge. 410-228-2520
S.T. McQuay & Son Shipyard. Wittman. 410-745-5530
Severn Marine Services, Inc. Knapps Narrows, Tilghman. 410-886-2159
Swan Creek Marina, Inc. 410-639-7813
Yacht Maintenance Co., Inc. 101 Hayward Street, Cambridge. 410-228-8878
The Sailing Emporium. 21144 Green Lane. Rock Hall. 410-778-1342
Gary James Boatworks. Hudson. 410-221-0744
Wikander's Marine Services. Allen. 410-749-9521
Black Dog. 201 River Road. Denton. 410-479-3355
Delmarva Marine. U.S. Rte. 13 By-Pass. Princess Anne. 410-651-1568
Greg Neck Boat Yard, Inc. Greg Neck Road. Galena. 410-648-5173

Chester River Marine Services. 7501 Church Hill Road. Chestertown. 410-778-2240

Cutts & Case. Tilghmann Street. Oxford. 410-226-5416
Classic Crafts. 846 Port Street. Easton. 410-818-0881
Haven Harbour Marina. MD Rte. 20 and Swan Creek, Rock Hall. 410-778-6697
Sutphins Varnishing. 22601 Pot Pie Road. Wittman. 410-745-6371
Island View Marina. Kent Island. 410-643-2842
Bay Bridge Marina. 357 Pier One Road. Stevensville. 410-643-3162
Brickhouse Yacht Yard, Inc. 910 Kentmorr Road. Stevensville. 410-643-1411
Kentmorr Harbour Marina. 410-643-0029
Knapp's Narrows Marina & Yacht Center. 410-886-2720
Lippincott Marine.Grasonville. 410-827-9300
Rick's Marine Service. 5000 Piney Neck Road. Rock Hall. 410-639-7367
Rock Hall Marine Railway. 5676 Hawthorne Avenue. Rock Hall. 410-639-2263
South Narrows Boat Works. 1807 Crab Alley Drive. Chester. 410-604-BOAT
Chesapeake Yacht Systems. 105 Evans Avenue. Grasonville. 410-827-0468

Boat Builders

Cutts & Case. Tilghmann Street, Oxford. 410-226-5416
Campbell's Bachelor Point. 26106A Bachelors Harbor. Oxford. 410-226-5592
Campbell's Town Creek Boatyard. 109 Myrtel Avenue. Oxford. 410-226-0213
Maynard Lowery. Tilghman Island. 410-745-5530
Carman Boats. Holland Crossing Road. Marion. 410-623-2628

Mathews Brothers

Mathews Brothers. 95 Walsh Way. Denton. 410-479-9720
Evans Boatbuilders. Crisfield. 410-968-3396
Copper-Nickel Boat Company Ltd. 9946 Deal Island Road. Deal Island. 410-784-2292
Allen Boatbuilders. 2242 Jenkins Creek Road. Cambridge. 410-476-3655
Dettling Yacht Co. 408 Brookletts Avenue. Easton. 410-822-1977
Nautor. Oxford. 410-226-5188

Yacht Dealers/Brokers

Oxford Yacht Agency. 317 South Morris Street. Oxford. 410-226-5454
Atlantic Coast Yacht Sales, Inc. 20838 Rock Hall Avenue. Rock Hall. 410-639-2050
Bay Bridge Marina. Kent Island. 410-643-3162
Eastern Shore Yacht Brokerage. 23143 Buck Neck Road. Chestertown. 410-778-6699
Gratitude Yachting Center. 5990 Lawton Avenue, Rock Hall. 410-639-7111
OBY Yacht Sales. Oxford. 410-226-0100
The Sailing Emporium, Inc. Rock Hall. 410-778-1342
Tred Avon Yacht Sales, Inc. Bachelor Harbor Marina. Oxford. 410-226-5000
Budd's Sales & Service. Warwick Road. Secretary. 410-943-4288

Chester River Marine Services Ltd. 7501 Church Hill Road. Chestertown. 410-778-2240
Island Yacht Brokers. 206 Piney Narrows Road. Chester. 410-643-3131
North Atlantic Mariner Group. 357 Pier One Road. Stevensville. 410-643-5400
Clark's Landing Boat Sales. Grasonville. 410-827-6600
Warehouse Creek Yacht Sales, Inc. 3020 Kent Narrows Way S. Grasonville. 410-643-7878
Sassafras Harbor Marina. 2 George Street. Georgetown. 888-221-5022
Reynolds Yacht Sales. Rte. 213. Gerogetown. 410-648-5347
Sailing Associates, Inc. Georgetown. 410-275-8171
Bayport Yachts. 415 Piney Narrows Road. Chester. 410-643-8100
Nautilus Yacht Sales. Skipjack Cove Yachting Resort. Georgetown. 410-275-1100
William A. Reynolds Yacht Sales. Georgetown Yacht Basin. Georgetown. 410-648-5347
Chester River Boat Sales. Rte. 301 and 544. Millington. 800-599-2628
Gootee's Marine. 1439 Hoopers Island Road. Church Creek. 410-397-3122
Tidewater. 1114 Talbot Street. St. Michael's. 410-745-5678
Island Yacht Brokers. Kent Narrows West. Chester. 410-643-3131
Winters Yacht Sales. 762 Kimberly Way. Stevensville. 410-643-6866
Lower Shore Yacht Sales. 4020 Crisfield Highway. Crisfield. 410-968-3427
Bollard Yachts. 410-226-0390

Yacht Charters

Compass Charters. Rock Hall. 410-639-7140
Southern Cross Charters. Chestetown. 410-778-4460
Gratitude Yachting Center. Rock Hall. 410-639-7111
Great River Yacht Charters. Rock Hall. 410-639-2166
Yachts Unlimited. Great Oak. 410-810-1726
Oxford Sailing Charters. Oxford. 410-226-0038
B&B Yacht Charters. Kent Island. 410-643-1529
C&C Charters. 506 Kent Narrows North. Grasonville. 410-827-7888
Cruise Adventures. 710 Oyster Cove Drive. Grasonville. 410-827-7535

Sailmakers

Cambridge Canvas & Sail Loft. 311 High Street, Cambridge. 410-228-7414
St. Michael's Sails 605 S. Talbot Street. St. Michael's. 410-745-3311
Meade Breese. 5680 S. Main Street. Rock Hall. 410-639-2646
North Sails. 208 E. Pier Street. Oxford. 410-226-5721

Kent Island Canvas Works. 210 Island Plaza. Stevensville. 410-643-9594

Electronic Supplies, Engine Parts and Service

Mid-Shore Electronics. 101 Hayward Street, Cambridge. 410-228-7335
Haven Harbour Marina. Rock Hall. 410-778-6697
Martek of Maryland, Inc/Kent Island. Bay Bridge Marina, Kent Island. 410-643-6888
Oxford Boatyard. 410-226-5101
The Sailing Emporium, Inc. Rock Hall. 410-778-1342
Yacht Maintenance Co., Inc. Cambridge. 410-228-8878
R&D Boat Supply. 22 Washington Street. Cambridge. 410-228-0674
Lighthouse Marine Engine Service. 410-758-2223
Tidewater Yacht Sales. 1114 Talbot Street. St. Michael's. 410-745-5678

Boat Surveyors

Independent Marine Survey. 5715 Ross Neck Road. Cambridge. 410-221-1108
Chris Oliver Marine engine Surveyor. 205 Oregon road. Stevensville. 410-643-1545

Boat Models

Anything Wood. 27710 Glebe Road. Easton. 410-820-9203
Model Boats by John Into. Wittman. 410-745-5954
Talbot Ship Shop. 211 N. Talbot Street. St. Michael's. 410- 745-6268
Wye River Models.Queenstown. wrm@crosslink.net
Peggy's Gifts. 413 S. Talbot. St. Michael's

Special Shops for Marine Hardware, Supplies, Clothing and Nautical Items

Oxford Boatyard. 402 E. The Strand. Oxford. 410-226-5101
Campbell's Bachelor Point Yacht Co. 26106A Bachelors Harbor. Oxford. 410-226-5592
St. Michael's Town Dock Marina. 800-678-8980

R&D Boat Supplies. Cambridge. 410-228--674
Sid Johnson Marine.301 Muir Street. Cambridge. 410-228-4820
Fairbank Tackle Shop. Knapp's Narrows. Tilghman
Arby's General Store. Main Street. Wenona
Easton Maritime Antiques, Inc. 27 S. Harrison Street, Easton
Talbot Street Ship Shop. 211 N. Talbot Street. St. Michael's
The Book Bank. Tilghman Island. 410-886-2230
Captain's Wheel Ltd. 405 S. Talbot Street. St. Michael's
A&M Marine Supplies. 116 Station Lane. Grasonville. 410-827-7409
Clarence Sterling & Son. 1012-1014 West Main Street. Crisfield. 410-968-1222
L. Forbush & Sons. 1000 W. Main Street. Crisfield
The Sailing Emporium, Inc. Rock Hall. 410-778-1342
Chester River Marine Services, Ltd. 7501 Church Hill Road. Chestertown. 410-778-2240
Fred Quimby's Marine. 9295 Ocean Gateway. Easton. 410-822-8107
L&B Marine Supply. Stevensville. 410-643-3600
Skipjack Landing Marine Center. 1804 Crab Alley Drive. Chester. 410-643-2694
Crockett Brothers Ships Store. 202 Banks Street. Oxford. 410-226-5113
Sailor of St. Michael's. 214 Talbot Street. St. Michael's. 410-745-2580
Harbor Shop. Georgetown Yacht Basin. Georgetown. 410-648-5112
Gateway Marina & Ship's Store. 1606 Marina Drive. Trappe. 410-476-3304
Bay Country Shop. 2709 Ocean Gateway. Cambridge. 410-221-0700
Chesapeake Outdoors. 1707 Main Street. Chester. 410-604-2500
Winchester Creek Outfitters. 303 Winchester Creek Road. Grasonville. 410-827-7000

Cruises on the Bay or Rivers

Schooner Sultana. Chestertown. 410-778-5954
Skipjack H.M. Krentz. Tilghman Island. 410-745-6080
Skipjack Rebecca Ruark. Tilghman Island. 410-886-2176
Nathan of Dorcester Skipjack Cruises. Long Wharf. Cambridge. 410-228-7141
River Cruises. Easton Point Landing. Easton. 410-822--2206
St. Michael's Lady. St. Michael's Town Dock. 410-745-5776
Cambridge Lady. Cambridge. 410-221-0776
Channel Charter Historical Cruises. Cambridge. 410-228-1645
All Aboard Charters. Knapps Narrows, Tilghman. 410-745-6022
Huntress Charters. Tilghman Island. 410-310-6619
Lady Patty Sail Charter. Tilghman. 410-886-2215
Wild Duck Charters. Chester. 410-643-7200
Little Boat Rentals. Easton Point. 800-221-1523

Patriot Cruises, Inc. Navy Point, St. Michael's. 410-745-3100
Smith Island Cruises. Crisfield. 410-425-2771
Tangier Island Cruises. Crisfield. 410-968-2338
Captain Jason. Crisfield. 410-425-5931
Island Belle. Crisfield. 410-968-1118
The Sailing Emporium, Inc. Rock Hall. 410-778-1342
St. Michael's Town Dock Marina. 800-678-8980
Pintail Point. Carmichael Road. 410-827-7029
Dockside Express. St. Michael's. 410-886-2643
Dorothy Megan. Secretary. 410-943-4689. This paddle boat provides cruises and dining.
Miss Claire. 64 Front Street. Chesapeake City. 410-885-5088
Blue Crab. Rock Hall. 800-256-3270
Chester River Cruises. 410-758-0277
The Kathryn. Rock Hall. 410-639-9902
Choptank Riverboat Company. Secretary. 410-943-4775

Fishing Charters

Harrison's Chesapeake Inn & Sportfishing Center. Tilghman. 410-886-2121
Fisherman's Charters. 3032 Kent Narrows Way. Grasonville. 410-827-8272
Dickie Webster. Deal Island. 410-784-2-53
All Aboard Charters. Tilghman. 410-745-6022
TideRunner Fishing Charter. Easton. 410-822-3474
Chesapeake Bay Charter Fishing. Rock Hall. 410-639-7507
Gunsmoke Charters. Rock Hall. 410-639-7127
Charter Boat Dawn II. Rock Hall. 410-639-2966
Chester River Marine Services Ltd. Chestertown. 410-778-2240
Captain Walton Benton. Wenona. 410-651-1762
Eastern Shore Bass Fishing. Snow Hill. 410-632-1431
Capt. Harry Nauman. Deal Island. 410-784-2690
Firth Charter Service. Trappe. 410-476-5227
Capt. Larry Tawes. Hebron. 410-546-3968
Capt. Ben Parks. Cambridge. 410-228-7837
Double A Charter Fishing. 6311 Suicide Bridge Road. Hurlock. 410-943-1124
Sawyer Fishing Charters & Tours. Hoopers Island. 410-397-3743
Tide Runner Fishing Charters. Hoopers Island. 410-397-FISH
Sassy Lady. Church Creek. 410-397-3578
Sawyer Fishing Charters. Church Creek. 410-397-3743
Striker Charters. Church Creek. 410-397-3234
Joint Venture Charters. Cambridge. 410-228-7837

Stony Cove Charters. Cambridge. 410-228-3552
Head Boat & Charter Boat Fishing. Crisfield. 410-957-2151
Prime Time II. Crisfield. 410-968-0074
Capt. John Bridges. Tilghman Island. 410-822-1838
Sea Dux Outfitters. Chestertown. 410-778-4362
Captain Paul Benton. Chance. 410-784-2343
Captain Bill Weiland. Chance. 410-784-2304
Captain. Stan Daniels. Wenona. 410-784-2693
Chelsea Lynn Charters. St. Michael's. 410-745-0044
Traveller II. Rock Hall. 410-639-7420
Capt. Fletch. Worton 410-810-2941
Capt. Fletcher. Rock Hall. 410-778-4022
Capt. Gears. Worton. 410-778-4767
Capt. Newberry. Chestertown. 410-778-4438
Capt. Price. Rock Hall. 410-639-7928
Capt. Ritchie. Rock Hall. 410-639-7063
Capt. Woodfield. Rock Hall. 410-778-3669
Capt. Gatling. Worton. 410-778-3191
Capt. Bob Gibson. Rock Hall. 410-778-9424
Capt. Jetton. Rock Hall. 410-639-7127
Capt. Manley. Rock Hall. 410-639-2966
Capt. Simns. Rock Hall. 410-639-2966
Carrie Ellen Charter Boat. Madison. 410-228-9294
Double AA II. Hurlock. 410-943-1124
Ell-Tom Charters. Woolford. 410-228-0879
Miss Pritch Charters. Taylor's Island. 410-397-3194
Capt. Mark Galasso. Grasonville. 410-827-5635
Grabacrab Charters. Harris Crab House. Grasonville. 410-758-1837
Captain's Pride Charters. Centreville. 410-758-3107
Pintail Point Charters. 5111 Pintail Point Farm Lane. Queenstown. 410-827-7029
Capt. E. Meredith Boat Charter. 3227 Main Street. Grasonville. 410-827-7737
Tuna the Tide Charter Service. 404 Greenwood Creek Lane. Grasonville. 410-827-5635
Eastern Shore Bass Fishing. 6661 Snow Hill Road. Snow Hill. 410-632-1431

Boat Rentals & Charters

Gratitude Yachting Center. Rock Hall. 410-639-7111
St. Michael's Town Dock Marina, Inc. 800-678-8980
Little Boat Rentals. 846 Port Street. Easton. 410-819-0881
Dividing Creek Canoe Rentals, Pocomoke City. 410-957-0858

Island Boat Rentals. 204 Queen Anne Road. Stevensville. 410-827-4777
Chester River Cruises. Chestertown. 410-778-2069
Eastern Neck Boat Rentals. Eastern Neck Island. 410-639-7100
Knee Deep Water Sports. Rolphs Wharf. 410-810-0514
Schnaitman's Boat Rental. Wye Mills. 410-827-7663
Cambridge Sailing Centre. 514 Poplar Street. Cambridge. 410-228-5525
Blue Crab. Rock Hall. 800-256-3270
Day Cruise Annapolis to Rock Hall. 410-268-7600
Dreamweaver Cruises. Georgetown. 877-599-3555
The Kathryn. Rock Hall. 410-639-9902
North American Sailing. Rock Hall. 410-639-9094
Compass Charters. Rock Hall
Sailing Emporium. Rock Hall. 410-778-1342
Southern Cross Charters. Great Oak. 410-778-4460
Yachts Unlimited. Great Oak. 410-810-1726

Kayaks/Canoes

Chesapeake Bay Kayaks. Neavitt. 410-745-5668
Island Kayaks. Tilghman. 410-886-2083
Pocomoke River Canoe Company. Snow Hill. 410-632-3971
Skipjack Cove Kayak Adventures. Skipjack Cove Yachting Resort. Georgetown. 800-BOATSLIP
Chester River Kayak Adventures. Rock Hall. 410-639-2001
Chester River Boat Rental. Chestertown. 410-778-224-
East Neck Boat Rentals. Rock Hall. 410-639-7100
Swan Haven. Rock Hall. 410-639-2527
Swan Haven Rentals. Rock Hall. 410-639-2527
Blackwater Paddle & Pedal. 4303 Bucktown Road. Cambridge. 410-901-9255
Chesapeake Water Sports and Outfitters. 514 Poplar Street. Cambridge. 410-288-5525
Tangier Sound Outfitters. Crisfield. 410-968-1803
Croaker Boat Rentals. Crisfield. 410-968-3644

Water Taxis

Kent Narrows Water Taxi. 200 Drake Lane. Chester. 410-212-4070
St. Michael's Harbor Shuttle. 410-924-2198

Sailing Schools

Maryland School of Sailing & Seamanship. 21035 Spring Cove Road, Rock Hall. 410-639-7030

Local Sailing Publications

Spin Sheet. Annapolis. 410-216-9309
Chesapeake Bay Magazine. 1819 Bay Ridge Avenue. Annapolis. 410-263-2662
Cruising World Magazine. 105 Eastern Avenue. Annapolis. 410-263-2484
Soundings Publication. 326 First Street. 410-263-2386
U.S. Naval Institute. U.S. Naval Academy. 410-224-3378
PassageMaker, The Trawler and Ocean Motorboat Magazine. Horn Point Marina. 888-487-2952
Tiller Publishing. PO Box 447-A. St. Michael's. 410-745-3750
The Mariner. 500 S. Main Street. Elkton. 410-287-9430
Nor'Easter. 102 Old Mill Plaza. Northeast. 1-800-884-7081
Chesapeake Life.1040 Park Ave., Suite 200. Baltimore

Special Organizations/ Trade Associations

Chesapeake Bay Foundation. 162 Prince George Street. Annapolis. 410-268-8816
Marine Trade Association of Maryland. Port Annapolis Marina. 7074 Bembe Beach Road. 410-269-0741
Chesapeake Region Accessible Boating Organization (CRAB) presents sailing opportunities for persons with or without disabilities. They have "Summer Sail Free" on the fourth Sunday of the month May to September. 410-974-2628

Well Known Eastern Shore Sailors Past and Present

The watermen – all of them

Stephen Decatur was born in Berlin. He entered the navy as a midshipman in 1798. From 1804-05 he fought against pirates in the Mediterranean and the British during the War of 1812.

Hal Roth and his wife, St. Michael's, have circled the globe by boat, and written a number of books about their travels.

Chester Baum, Oxford was a much-admired racer, raconteur, scholar and gentleman.

Andrew Watters, Oxford sails in the U.S. Optimist class.

Chris Wilson, Oxford competed in the Balboa National Pram Championship in June 1999 and is also a member of the Optimist Team.

Tad DuPont is the owner of *Nicole* which has raced in a number of Annapolis-Newport and Newport-Bermuda races.

Sylvain Barrielle is a three time America's Cup racer for the French team. He has also competed in other classes and has done the Annapolis- Bermuda race.

Judge John North owns several log canoes. One was built by his uncle, John B. Harrison, in 1931. Others date to the late 1800s and were built by his great-grandfather, William S. Covington. They include *Island Bird* and *Island Blossom,* which can still seen be racing.

Prominent Boat Builders Past and Present

Robert Dawson Lambdin (Captain Bob) was a well known shipbuilder in St. Michael's. The shipyard was started by his father at Long Wharf and Mulberry Street in 1830. George Lambdin later built log canoes.

John B. Harrison, Tilghman Island built log canoes and power boats. He built *J.B. Harrison* in 1890, probably the largest log canoe ever built, *Jay Dee* for John D. Williams in 1931 and *Flying Cloud* for Johnson Grymes of Oxford in 1932.

William Sidney Covington, Tilghman Island built log canoes including *Island Bird* in 1882 and *Island Blossom* for Captain Will Myers of Oxford in 1892. His other canoes included *Island Belle, Island Beauty, and Island Bride*

Thomas Smyth, Chestertown was a famous 18th c boat builder.

Tom Young of Young's Creek, Eastern Shore of Virginia, built a number of skipkacks – *the Bernice Jewell*, the *Mary W. Somers*, the *Rew Brothers*, the

Claude W. Somers, the *Annie Lee*, the *Lena Rose*, the *Joy Parks*, and the *Lola*. Even though Mr. Young was from Virginia, he is mentioned because many of his boats ended up on the Eastern Shore of Maryland.

John Branford, Fishing Island (born 1855) produced a large number of bugeyes and skipjacks, including the *Lizzie J. Cox*.

Oliver Duke of Royal Oak built bugeyes and then skipjacks.

Maynard Lowery was born and raised on Tilghman Island. He has built many catboats and workboats. He now has a fleet of boats at his boatyard among them *Kit Kat*, *Catnipper* and *Catnapper*.

Maynard Lowery

Jim Richardson lived near Cambridge on LeCompte Bay. His mother was descended from the LeCompte family who came to the area in 1650. The Richardson family are known to have opened a boatyard in the 1600s in

Baltimore, and then moved to the Eastern Shore for the timber. Mr. Richardson built skipjacks such as *Sweepstakes* for Howard Chapelle; the ship replica of the *Dove,* one of the original boats to sail to America from England; the *Adventurer*, a coastal trading ketch; the *Jenny Norman*, a smaller version of a bugeye, and numerous other boats.

Moses Geoghegan built the *J.T. Leonard*, the last Chesapeake Bay built sloop in 1882 on Taylor's Island. Her last year of working the Bay was in 1968.

Ralph Wiley was a noted boatbuilder in the 1920s at Cutts and Case Boatyard, Oxford. The Cutts family runs Cutts and Case, and produces some of the loveliest wooden boats on the Eastern Shore, and for that matter anywhere. The site of Cutts and Case Boatyard in Oxford has been a boatyard since the 1600s.

T. Kirby, St. Michael's built schooners in the later 1800s, including the *Bohemia,* which carried wheat, corn, fertilizer and lumber on the Chesapeake. Thomas Kirby & Sons built the bugeye *Dan.*

Bronza M. Parks of Wingate in Dorchester County, a former oyster dredger, built several skipjacks, including the *Lady Katie*, *Martha Lewis* and *Rosie Parks*.

Harry Sinclair and his son M. Price Sinclair of Oxford built the log canoe *Mystery.*

Charles Tarr of St. Michael's built the log canoe *Magic.*

Otis Lloyd of Salisbury built the bugeye *Norm*a.

Special Museums

<u>Chesapeake Bay Maritime Museum.</u> Navy Point. St. Michael's. This the most comprehensive museum in the region on the history and culture of the Chesapeake Bay and its boats.
<u>Richardson Maritime Museum.</u> Locust and High Streets. Cambridge. The museum is named for Jim Richardson, a noted boatbuilder. It has a lot of history and artifacts on wooden boats.
<u>The Watermen's Museum</u>. Rock Hall. This very small museum plans to expand and is currently undegoing fundraising for this.
<u>Brannock Maritime Museum.</u> 210 Talbot Avenue. Cambridge
<u>Upper Bay Museum.</u> Walnut Street. North East. The museum has a large collection of antique marine engines and other items related to the Bay.

Noted Maritime Painters

There are many people who have painted maritime scenes on the Eastern Shore. However a number are not from the Eastern Shore. Some of the better known painters are John Morton Barber from Richmond, Keith Whitlock from Salisbury, The Traveling Brushes, N. Benjamin Dize, Ned Ewell, Richard Harryman from Annapolis, Clark S. Marshall, Bruce Etchison, David Atkins from Rock Hall, and Don R. Tate to mention a few.

Louis Fuechter was one of the most noted painters of the Eastern Shore. He was born in Baltimore in 1885, and worked for the Kirk silver company. He helped to design the silver service for the *Maryland.* He spent time at Kemp's Boarding house, Wade's Point, now the Wade's Point Inn, taking the steamer *Cambridge* from Baltimore to Claiborne. He got to know the Eastern Shore boats through the log canoe *Louise*, named for Louise Kemp and built by James Lowery of Tilghman Island. His paintings now hang in museums and private collections and depict not only the boats of the Eastern Shore, but wildlife as well.

Did You Know?

The state boat of Maryland is the skipjack.

83 skipjacks were known to have been built in Dorchester County. *The Nathan of Dorchester* was completed in 1994. The Dorchester Skipjack Committee, a nonprofit organization, offers educational programs.

The longest skipjack built was the *Robert L. Webster* for Eldon Willing of Chance. She was built in 1915 at Oriole, near Deal Island, and was sixty feet in length.

The *Rebecca T. Ruark* was the last sloop hull to work the oyster bars under sail. She was built in 1886 and is presently owned by Capt. Wade Murphy, Jr of Tilghman Island.

Somerset County produced the most bugeyes, a centerboard boat built of hewn logs and powered by three sails on two raked masts. The last sailing bugeye built was the *Edna E. Lockwood*, now at the Chesapeake Bay Maritime Museum in St. Michael's.

The Maryland Watermen's Monument is expected to be completed in 2000 and will be placed in Kent Narrows. The design was rendered by Tilghman Hemsley.

Captain Edward Trippe of Dorchester County introduced the steamboat to the Chesapeake. Amazingly enough the first boat *Chesapeake* began her runs in 1813 as the British advanced up the Bay during the War of 1812. The *Eagle* was the first steamship to run between Baltimore and Norfolk.

The Schooner Sultana project, based in Chestertown, is building the *Sultana,* a reproduction of a vessel that would have plied the waters of the Chesapeake Bay two hundred years ago. The staff teaches children and adults about the history, culture and environment of the Chesapeake Bay region. *Sultana* is expected to be completed in the spring of 2001.

Albert Brown of Wenona is the fourth generation of the Brown family to make sails.

The Annual Chesapeake Bay Championship Workboat Regatta was held on the Bay from 1921-31. The regatta was organized by Peter C. Chambliss, city editor of the Baltimore Sun, which sponsored the races. The first race was held in 1921 off Claiborne. Other races were held off Bay Ridge, Crisfield, Solomons, Oxford, Bay Shore, Deal Island and Piney Point.

The *Tolchester* was built as the *St. Johns* in Wilmington, Delaware in 1878. She was brought to Baltimore in 1933 and renamed the *Tolchester.* The steamship took passengers from Baltimore to Tolchester. She burned in Baltimore in 1941. Another steamer taking passengers to Tolchester was the *Emma Giles*. Her last season was in 1936.

The first official club sanctioned powerboat race in the Chesapeake was held in Cambridge in 1911.

Carroll Thamert of Neavitt is the fourth generation of his family to be a waterman. His great-great grandfather emigrated to the United States as a fisherman. His grandfather Harrison was a shipbuilder.

Robert M. Brittain became the captain of the *Sultana* of Chestertown in May 2004. Even though he was raised in England he moved to the States in 1980. He has served on the *Lady Maryland*, *Woodwind*, *Woodwind II* and the *Martha Lewis.* He has also sailed on the original *Pride of Baltimore* and on the maiden voyage of the newer *Pride of Baltimore.*

Chapter Five

Waterfowl, Wildlife and the Sporting Life

Ward Museum of Waterfowl Art

A guidebook to the Eastern Shore would not be complete if waterfowl were not mentioned. This Bay region has been on migration paths for thousands of years, with numerous rivers, creeks, brackish wetlands and marshland to attract many species of wildlife.

The area offers wood carvers, bird watchers, animal lovers and hunters a chance to see wildlife in beautiful natural settings along the Bay, its rivers and creeks.

A number of different birds can be spotted on the Eastern Shore. These include – the canvasback duck, Canada geese, loon, swans, eagles, duck, cormorants, hawks, osprey, bald eagles, great blue heron, pelican, terns and cattle egret.

Trumpeter swans had been very common in the region until recently. Several years ago the Migratory Bird Program introduced ultra-light aircraft to teach the trumpeter swans to be led back to the Chesapeake Bay.

The northern diamond terrapin have been considered a delicacy for many years, and were shipped up and down the coasts to clubs, restaurants and fish markets. By about 1920 the supply had almost been completely depleted and laws were passed to limit the catch. Today they have come back, though not in great numbers. The Chesapeake Bay is noted for oysters and crab, but fish swim in abundance too. Fish include rockfish, shad, bluefish and bass.

Decoys

The Eastern Shore is renowned for its decoys and bird carvings. The most famous show occurs in November in Easton. Master decoy makers come from around the world to show off their prized carvings.

William I. Tawes in his book *Creative Bird Carving* traces the history of this craft back to early Egyptian history when wooden carvings were found in the tombs of the pharaohs and others, including Hammarubi. In this country the Indians also carved wood for utensils, totem poles, and included birds and other animals. Gods were often represented as birds.

Decoys were used by the Indians and later the settlers to this area. Unlike in Europe where game belonged to the Crown and only royalty could hunt, everyone could hunt in America. The Indians hunted in log canoes using reed decoys and arrowheads. The early settlers began to use large guns. These and lights were eventually outlawed for hunting. During the 1800s rail and ship transportation permitted rapid transport to growing markets for wildfowl and seafood.

Carving is a beautiful and unique art. A person has to observe some of these carvings so closely only to realize it is not the real bird. Each feather, each marking is so delicately carved and painted. A true master carver does not come about his work in a brief time, but learns to observe every detail of the model to be carved. Decoys have regional characteristics. One of the best ways to truly understand this is to attend the Waterfowl Festival held annually in Easton, or any of a number of other festivals and shows. However, the Easton show ranks on top nationally and internationally.

The Ward Foundation was chartered in 1968. In 1971 the Ward World Championship Wildfowl Carving Competition was first held in Ocean City. 2000 marks the 30th anniversary of this event.

From 1980 to 1987 a world Championship featured a feather carving contest where the artist submitted a real and carved feather for comparison. Some samples of these can be seen at the Ward Museum of Waterfowl Art in Salisbury.

Noted Bird Carvers:

The most famous carvers were Lemuel and Steve Ward Crisfield. Lem did the painting of the carvings and Steve the carving. These two men were barbers, but carving became more than a pastime as their craft became known. The Ward Foundation and the Ward Museum of Waterfowl Art honor these two men.

Other noted carvers come from across the United States, Canada and elsewhere, but they are not mentioned here, even though a number of them have won awards at the various shows and festivals on the Eastern Shore. Some of these carvers are now deceased, but memories of them linger in museums and private collections.

Lemuel (1896-1985) and Steven (1895-1976) Ward, Crisfield
Tom (1820-66) and Edward (1856-1937) Parsons, Oxford
William I. Tawes, Crisfield
Noah B. Sterling, Crisfield (1870-1950)
J. Lloyd Sterling (1880-1964), Crisfield. Mr. Sterling worked very closely with the Wards.
L. Travis Ward, Sr. Crisfield (1863-1926)
Larry Tawes. Sr. Salisbury
Larry Tawes, Jr. Hebron
Richard Tilghman. Talbot County
Edmund Hardcastle. Talbot County
Charles Joiner. Chestertown
Edward J. Phillips, Golden Hill (1901-64)
Capt. Jessie A. Urie, Rock Hall (1901-1978)
William T. (1907-1983) and Francis Elliott (1907-1995), Easton
Lloyd Tyler, Crisfield (1898-1971)
J. Newnam Valliant, Bellevue
Joseph Liener. Wittman
Bernie White. Hoopers Island
Paul F. Nock. Salisbury
General C. Braddock deGavre, from the Virginia Eastern Shore
Oliver Lawson. Crisfield
Robert D. Lambdin. St. Michael's
Frank Cockey. Stevensville
Josiah Travers, Vienna
Paul Marshall. Smith Island
Bennett Scott, Berlin. 1974 Shootin' Stool Champion
Capt. John Glen. Rock Hall (1876-1954)
Rich Smoker. Crisfield
Habbart Dean. Bishopville
J.D. Sprankle, Kent Island, was once a minor league pitcher.
Ira Hudson. Chincoteague
Russell Allen, Jr. Trappe
Knute R. Bartug. Salisbury
Dan Brown. Hebron

Bernard N. Burns. Easton
Ed and Esther Burns. St. Michael's
Lu Fisher. Queenstown
Oliver Lawson. Crisfield
Ernie Muehlmatt. Salisbury
Ronald Rue. Cambridge
D. Bennett Scott. Berlin

Waterfowl Painters:

Lem Ward of Crisfield was not only a master carver along with his brother Steve, but also painted waterfowl scenes. Other waterfowl painters from the Eastern Shore include Keith Whitlock, Salisbury; Peter Hanks, Easton; the Traveling Brushes; and Kevin Snelling, Cambridge.

Museums:

Ward Museum of Waterfowl Art. 909 S. Shumaker Drive. Salisbury. 410-742-4988. The museum opened in 1992 and is operated by the Ward Foundation, established in 1974. A gallery recreates the Ward brothers' workshop. The Championship Gallery houses winners of the Ward carving competition held in Ocean City each year.
Chesapeake Bay Maritime Museum. Navy Point, St. Michael's. 410-745-2916. One building is dedicated to waterfowl.
J. Millard Tawes Historical Museum. 3 Ninth Street. Crisfield. 410-968-2501. Some of the artwork is devoted to Steve and Lem Ward.
Upper Bay Museum. Walnut Street. North East. The museum has dispays of decoys and hunting implements.

Refuges

Blackwater National Wildlife Refuge. Rte 16, south of Cambridge
Wildlife Trust of North America at Horsehead Wetlands Center. 600 Discovery Lane. Grasonville. There are over 300 acres of beautiful marshland here. One can walk trails, visit the waterfowl research facility, or attend special events.
Horsehead Wetlands Center. Grasonville
Wye Island Natural Resources Management Area. Queenstown
Terrapin Nature Center. Stevensville
Adkins Arboretum. Hillsboro
Eastern Neck National Wildlife Refuge. Rock Hall. This refuge is 2,285 acres at the mouth of the Chester River on the Chesapeake Bay. Over 1,000 acres is brackish tidal marsh, 600 acres crops, 500 acres forest, 100 acres of grassland and 40 acres of open water impoundments. A number of different wildlife inhabit this pristine area.

Shops

The Wood Duck Shoppe and Gallery. 8374 Ocean Gateway. Easton
Delaware Sporting Gallery. Dover and Washington Streets. Easton
The Puddle Duck. 3019 Kent Narrows Way South. Grasonville
Watson's Wildlife Art Gallery. 928 South Division Street. Salisbury
Bay Country Shop.2709 Ocean Highway. Cambridge

Associations:

The Grand National Waterfowl Association. 411-B Dorchester Avenue. Cambridge. 410-228-0111. This organization sponsors tournaments, hunts and shoots.
Chesapeake Bay Foundation. The Karen Noonan Center for Environmental Studies. Bishop's Head
Ducks Unlimited, Talbot County Chapter. 19 Federal Street. Easton. 410-819-3005
Chesapeake Wildlife Heritage. 46 Pennsylvania Avenue. Easton. 410-822-5100

Waterfowl Festivals:

Waterfowl Festival. Easton. 410-822-4567. November. Events include master classes, carving demonstrations and exhibits, paintings and sculpture, retriever demonstrations, calling contests and various seminars.
Wildlife Exhibition & Sale. Chestertown. October. Carvers and exhibitors display their craft at this exhibit.
Upper Shore Decoy Show. North East. October
Floating Decoy Show. North East. Memorial Day week-end

Contests:

Federal Duck Stamp contest. 1-800-534-1400
Ward World Championship Wildfowl Carving Competition. Ocean City

Books:

Creative Bird Carving — William I. Tawes
Creative Sculpture — William I. Tawes
Chesapeake Bay Decoys — Robert H. Richardson

Alphabetical List of Cities, Towns and Villages

About the Author and Photographers

Katie Moose, born in Baltimore, is a descendant of the Clagett (Claggett) family of Maryland, and many old New England whaling families. She has lived in many of the U.S.' great architectural, historical and waterside gems besides Annapolis - New Castle, DE; Newport and Providence, RI; Cold Spring Harbor, NY; San Francisco; Philadelphia; Greenwich, CT; Alexandria, VA; Washington, DC; and New York City. She and her family also maintain homes on historic Nantucket Island.

Mrs. Moose is the co-author of "The Best of Newport"; author of "Annapolis: The Guidebook", "Eastern Shore of Maryland: The Guidebook", Maryland's Western Shore: The Guidebook" "Chesapeake's Bounty II", "Nantucket's Bounty", and New England's Bounty", and several publications on the fiber optic telecommunications business, and is a consultant on international business and protocol. Her hobbies include gourmet cooking, fine wines, history, sailing, genealogy, theology and travel.

George Moose, though raised in North Carolina has spent much time living on the Eastern Shore and twice in Annapolis. His love for the sea stems from the time he spent with Capt. Stanley Larrimore aboard the skipjack, the *Lady Katie*, now in Cambridge. His work at Fawcett Boat Supplies in Annapolis has brought him in touch with many of yachting's finest.

Mr. Moose has also learned to restore fine antiques, and with a degree in history, appreciates the significance of the Eastern Shore's history. He is an excellent sailor, gourmet chef, genealogist, and avid reader. However, his favorite pastime is photography when not fooling around in boatyards.

Order Form for Conduit Press Books

Please send me____ copies of Nantucket's Bounty @ $17.95

Please send me____ copies of New England's Bounty @ $17.95

Please send me ____ copies of Chesapeake's Bounty @ $16.95

Please send me____ copies of Chesapeake's Bounty II @ $17.95

Please send me____ copies of Annapolis: The Guidebook @ $13.95

Please send me____ copies of Eastern Shore of Maryland: The Guidebook @ $15.95

Please send me____ copies of Maryland's Western Shore: The Guidebook @ $15.95

Add postage first book @ $3.00____
Postage for each additional book to same address @ $1.00____
Gift wrap per book @$2.00____
Total Order______

- ❑ Check or money order enclosed
- ❑ Make check payable to Conduit Press
- ❑ Please personalize to:

Mail to:

Conduit Press
111 Conduit Street
Annapolis, MD 21401

Ship or deliver the Cookbooks and guidebooks to:

Name____

Address____

____

Telephone____

For further information please

- Call 410-280-5272
- Fax 410-263-5380
- E-mail:kamoose@erols.com